Penguin Books

A Woman's Place

1 0

Diana Souhami has worked in publishing as an editor and as a picture researcher. Her plays have been produced on television and radio and in fringe theatres in London. She has published articles and short stories and reviews fiction for the **New Statesman**, **City Limits**, and other magazines.

She devised and researched the British Council exhibition **A Woman's Place: The Changing Picture of Women in Britain**, which was previewed at the Royal Festival Hall in 1984 and is now being toured overseas. It is scheduled to be shown in thirty different countries. It was from that exhibition that this book developed.

Diana Souhami

Punk, London
photo: Derek W. Ridgers

A WOMAN'S PLACE:
THE CHANGING PICTURE OF WOMEN IN BRITAIN

Southend promenade   photo: Chris Steele-Perkins

Long jump
photo: Jürgen Schadeberg

Penguin Books Ltd,
Harmondsworth, Middlesex, England
Viking Penguin Inc.,
40 West 23rd Street, New York, New York 10010, U.S.A.
Penguin Books Australia Ltd,
Ringwood, Victoria, Australia
Penguin Books Canada LImited,
2801 John Street, Markham, Ontario, Canada L3R 1B4
Penguin Books (N.Z.) Ltd,
182–190 Wairau Road, Auckland 10, New Zealand

First published 1986

Designed by Richard Hollis

Typeset, printed and bound in Great Britain by
Hazell Watson and Viney Limited,
Member of the BPCC Group,
Aylesbury, Bucks

Typeset in Century Schoolbook
and Helvetica

Contents

Acknowledgements   6
Introduction   8

1. **'VOTES FOR WOMEN':**
   THE FIGHT FOR SUFFRAGE 1900–1928   13

2. **'FLINT AND ROSES. VERY ODD':**
   WOMEN'S WORK IN WARTIME   33

3. **'NOW MISS, YOU MUST NOT MAKE AUGUSTA A BLUE':**
   THE EDUCATION OF GIRLS   53

4. **LIFE BEYOND THE NAPPY BUCKET:**
   WOMEN AND THE FAMILY   69

5. **'PAY PEANUTS AND YOU GET MONKEYS':**
   WOMEN'S WORK   93

6. **'BRIDES, MUMS AND SIZZLERS':**
   IMAGE AND STEREOTYPING   115

7. **THE QUIET REVOLUTION:**
   PROTEST AND CHANGE   137

Select Bibliography   158
Index   159

Acknowledgements

This book is derived from an exhibition of the same title commissioned by the British Council in 1984. The exhibition was previewed at the Royal Festival Hall, London, and two versions of it are now being toured to thirty countries. It was researched and co-ordinated by Diana Souhami and designed and produced by Richard Hollis with the architects Sheila Bull and Jon Corpe. The photographs reproduced here are selected from among those used in the exhibition.

Many women contributed to the text of the exhibition on which the themes of this book are based. They include Sally Alexander, Anny Brackx, Harriett Gilbert, Judith Hunt, Ursula Huws, Jane Lewis, Maggie Millman, Jill Nicolls, Ann Oakley, Sue Owen, Lesley Rimmer, Joan Ruddock, Rosemary Stones, Mary Stott, Annmarie Turnbull, Valerie Walkerdine, Judith Williamson and Nancy Worcester. The research unit of the Equal Opportunities Commission provided advice on statistics, which are taken from the latest available sources.

**'A Woman's Place'
exhibition,
London 1984**
photo: Ben Johnson

Weavers, Lancashire photo: Daniel Meadows

Introduction

Pictures of women plaster the environment. Legs, breasts, hands, bottoms and smiles are displayed on advertising hoardings, in magazines, calendars and TV commercials. They belong to Ms Perfection and are used to sell a bemusing variety of objects – car tyres, potatoes, lawn-mowers, deodorants, prefabricated buildings, diamonds, videos and hair dyes. The serious newspapers give saturation coverage to images of the Queen, Margaret Thatcher and the Princess of Wales. The lesser tabloids show women as sizzlers, victims of crime or scandal, or as the wives of newsworthy men.

The selection of pictures in this book aims for a more diverse view. It shows the women who work in the factories, not the products they are urged to buy. It shows the suffragettes' struggle for the right to vote and the Greenham women's struggle for peace. It shows women working as deep-sea divers, fire fighters and bus drivers as well as domestic workers in and out of their homes. It shows women from Asia, the West Indies, Tyneside, the Home Counties, for all of whom Britain is their workplace and their home. These pictures give visual instances of contrast and of change: women workers crammed into a bustling hat factory at the turn of the century and women operating VDU screens in a high-tech neon-lit office; the relieved smile of a mother who has just given birth and the tense eyes of a woman queuing for the dole; a small girl absorbed in modelling clay and factory women checking tin cans – no doubt for pittance pay; a stripper in a dingy pub and women voting with a unanimous show of hands at a union meeting; the traditional marriage of a bride in white and a lone parent with her child; the rebellious style of punks and polite partakers of a church tea. From woman to woman the picture changes.

The photographs are grouped in seven themes: the struggle for franchise; the role of women in the two world wars; the evolution of education from its domestic science bias; changing concepts of family; women's work today relative to men's; the way women are portrayed in advertising, language and imagery, and the current movement of protest and reform. Any one of these issues is a specialist subject in itself, on which much of depth is now in print. The contributions needed to bring the reality of women's existence and achievements to our attention increase by the day. The text that accompanies the pictures is derived from other women's work. It gives brief factual substance to these themes. It shows the courage of the suffragists and suffragettes in their long campaign for votes for women and how that same spirit is shared by women activists now. It describes how women won the right to equal education and work opportunities with men and how those rights are thwarted by narrow assumptions of women's worth. It shows how, in 1918 and again in 1940, women exploded the domestic docile identity accorded them and worked as crane drivers, welders, coal heavers and shell turners at the government's behest. It gives evidence of the diverse nature of modern family life and the changed expectations of mothers, lovers and wives. It describes how advertisements, images and constructs of language are used to exclude, objectify and diminish the picture of women's achievements, hopes and goals.

The picture for women is changing, but in a push-pull way. Gains are won in legislation, then lost when national economic vagaries mean that women's jobs are the first to go. Fifty-one per cent of the population are women and yet they feel, as keenly as any minority group, the closed door of exclusion when it comes to equal opportunities. The cold facts of censuses, surveys and statistics show that women are still ingloriously excluded from the well-rewarded jobs, the decision-making echelons and most positions of privilege and power. Out of 625 members of parliament, 25 are women; of 78 High Court judges, three are women; less than one per cent of directors of public and large companies are women.

Young machinist, West Midlands
photo: Nick Hedges

Most women do paid work for nearly all their active lives, but they are process workers rather than supervisors, nurses not consultants, community lawyers not judges. The ghettos of female labour are the service sector and a few of the manufacturing industries, and women still earn on average only two thirds as much as men – the same ratio as in 1945. The domestic sphere is still propounded by many to be women's proper place. Historically, the bias of their education was designed to shape them into at best ladies of leisure and at worst servants of obsequy and self-effacement. Now, though ostensibly women are free and equal to follow the career of their choice, the home-centred myth still figures large. It is reinforced by advertising images, women's magazines and politicians embarrassed by endless dole queues. It shapes the sort of paid work that women do outside the home – cooking, cleaning, child care, nursing, teaching.

Old people's home, London
photo: Homer Sykes

But home is now for women a much transformed place. One in three marriages ends in divorce, one in three marriages is a remarriage for one or both partners. Thirteen per cent of children are born outside marriage. One family in nine is headed by a mother alone. The average married couple has 1·9 children, the average single mother 1·6. Increasing numbers of women live by themselves or with lovers or friends. The same woman lives in different ways at different stages of her life. Women's life expectation is 76 years – ten years longer than in the 1930s.

What these bald facts mean is that the old definitions of a woman's place no longer apply. Women not only desire equality and independence, they need it as their right and as an economic necessity. Such gains as there are have been won relatively recently. It was 1928 before women won the right to vote on the same basis as men, 1948 before they could take degrees from Cambridge University, 1956 when equal pay was introduced for women teachers and civil servants, 1968 when abortion was made legal in certain circumstances, 1969 before divorce was possible on the grounds of incompatibility rather than cruelty, desertion or insanity, 1974 when contraceptive advice and supplies were available free on the National Health Service, 1975 when sex equality legislation made it illegal to discriminate against women in work or education or to pay them less than men for doing equivalent work, and 1985 before an amendment to the Equal Pay Act said that equal pay should be given for work of equal value.

Legislation that outlaws sex discrimination and promotes financial, employment, educational and legal equality is vital to women if they are to get their rights. But it is useless if not implemented, and provision for its enforcement is worse than weak. The Equal Opportunities Commission (EOC) was set up to aid, review and help implement the Equal Pay and Sex Discrimination Acts. It has been described, to use a sexist image, as 'a rather wet, ladylike body, too concerned with holding its skirts down against the rude winds to have a go at entrenched masculine strongholds'.*

* **Guardian,** 19 March 1979, quoted in Ann Oakley, **Subject Women**, Fontana, 1982

In 1976, the year after the equality Acts, 1,742 applications for equal pay were made to Industrial Tribunals, of which 709 were heard and 213 upheld. Out of 243 alleged cases of sex discrimination, 119 were heard and 24 upheld. In 1984, out of 33 applications for equal pay, 17 were heard and 6 upheld, and out of 225 sex discrimination cases, 91 were heard and 40 upheld. The system of application is cumbersome and the outcome discouraging. Strong enforcement procedures are

Mary Stott and Dora Russell

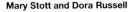

photo: Jill Posener

Checking tin cans, Cambridgeshire
photo: Carlos Guarita

10

Wallington ladies' cricket team
photo: Brenda Prince/Format

needed if equality legislation is to effect change and get women a fair deal.

Only one model of sex equality is on offer – one that says women should be equal to men. It is not suggested that men should become equal to women. Men make the rules and see women's traditional preoccupations as weaknesses, not strengths. But women have their doubts about the man-made social order, so the exclusion works two ways. Many women see the institutions of the Establishment – the army, the city, the law, the church – as arcane masculinist structures for which revision is long overdue. The bewigged judges, generals with their medals, and bosses and bankers in city suits, want their colleagues to be of the same class, colour, sex and style as themselves. For their part women are unattracted to the notion of wearing wigs and funny suits and promulgating theories and conventions to which they have no historical allegiance and in which they do not believe. Women want responsibility, fair pay and involvement at the decision-making level of society. They don't want necessarily to compromise themselves to achieve these goals.

Women are moving slowly towards ostensible equality with men. In small but growing numbers they are working in a wider range of professions. More expect men to share domestic chores and false assumptions about sexual identity are being challenged and discounted. Where women are changing fast is in the way they are organizing for themselves. It is in this area that a vision of liberation lies. Women's studies courses, consciousness-raising groups, counselling services, women's groups within the professions, politics and unions, feminist publishers, bookshops and libraries, campaign and protest groups, support networks, national committees and councils – all are snowballing. And women's publishing is now entrenched. Everything to do with women's position in society is discussed, analysed, written about and published by women and for women. Women painters, poets, musicians, scientists and philosophers of the past are being painstakingly exhumed. Their successors are asking for, and achieving, recognition while they live. This output and activity give evidence of a massive reappraisal, a quiet revolution.

Historically, women's agitation for change was directed at specific issues: the franchise, divorce reform, fertility control, education rights, the abolition of laws that entrenched inferior status and pay. Now the activity and agitation is directed at recreating their past and changing their opinion of themselves and their position in society. It is a groundswell of activity that gathers momentum all the time. There are no particular leaders. It is a grass-roots affair. No sophistry or political dissuasion will cause it to subside.

Such a movement among men seems unlikely. Their history, culture, achievements and failures are apparent everywhere. Quite where they go next is a problem for all. But the spread of the women's movement suggests that mothers, sisters, female work colleagues, lovers, wives and women friends are evolving into different kinds of women with wider expectations, more self-confidence and stronger attitudes and views. The chances are that in such a brave new world men will have to change too.

1.

'VOTES FOR WOMEN': THE FIGHT FOR SUFFRAGE 1900-1928.

photo: BBC Hulton

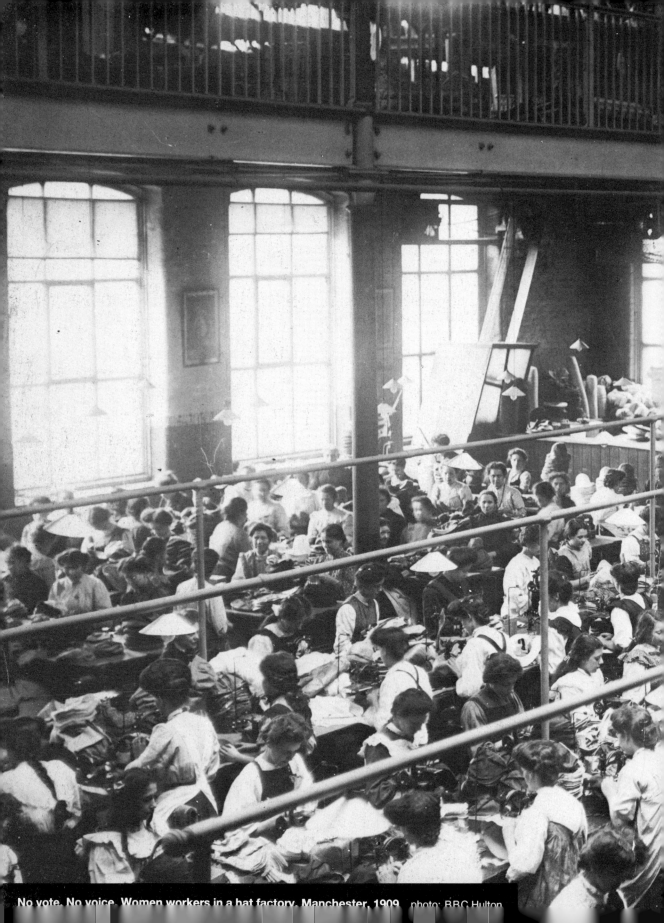

No vote. No voice. Women workers in a hat factory. Manchester, 1909. photo: BBC Hulton

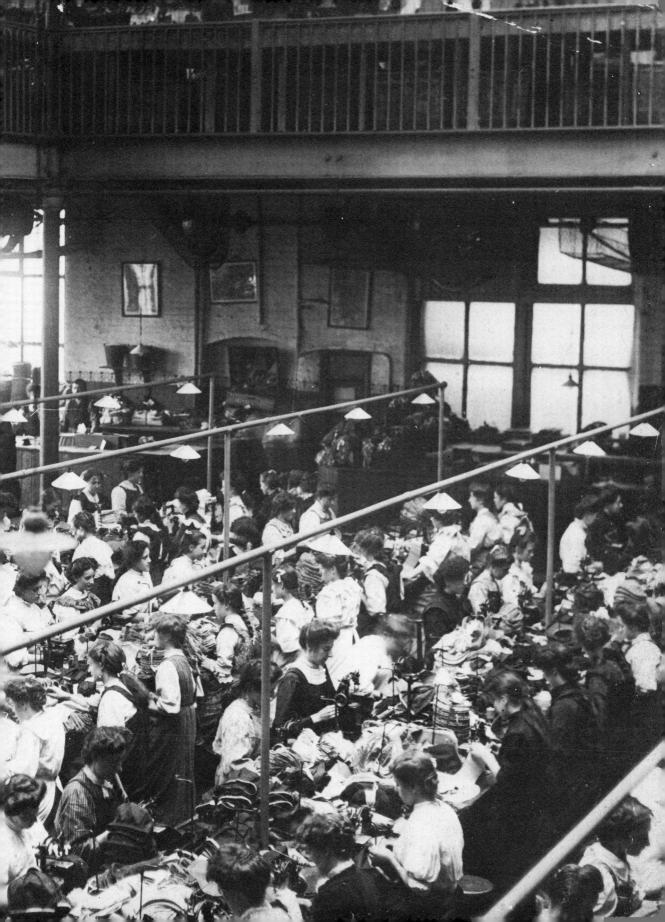

Married women over 30 won the right to vote in parliamentary elections in Britain in 1918. Ten years later the age discrimination was lifted and they got the vote on the same basis as men. The fact that women were until so recently denied any political voice is startling. The sub-text of that denial persists today. It has to do with assumptions about women's intellectual inferiority and domestic preoccupations, the arrogation of male power and privilege and men's lack of interest in women's views, achievements and abilities. Such unfairness is now vigilantly scrutinized, probed and exposed by women. Eighty years ago what they sought was a change in the law.

From the early 1900s on, the cause of women's suffrage was a flamboyant political issue. The extraordinary behaviour of the 'suffragettes', as members of the Women's Social and Political Union were called, and the wide propaganda of the 'suffragists' – the law-abiding campaigners – meant that everyone in the country knew of the fight. The Liberal government tried to duck it officially, but that did not stop people having an opinion. They could be for or against with certainty and ease. The idea of sexual equality might be revolutionary but, as presented, the solution was simple. Women either should, or should not, be allowed to vote. There were those who said yes out of fairmindedness, curiosity or apathy and those who said no out of conservatism, prejudice or fear.

To many women of the time the brazen acts of protest of these upper-class suffragettes seemed scandalous. Smashing windows and chaining yourself to the railings did not constitute ladylike behaviour. For hundreds of thousands more, the growing campaign reflected their anger at dependence, powerlessness, low pay and conventional limitations. Throughout the country local meetings were held in halls, drawing rooms, schools and chapels. In 1907 there was the first big public demonstration. Three thousand women marched from Hyde Park Corner to Exeter Hall with banners and placards. Similar processions took place in Manchester and Edinburgh. The idea of public demonstration of 'faith in the cause' caught on fast. It drew support from unionized working women, especially textile workers in the north-west of England. The universal slogan was 'Votes for Women'.

The law-abiding constitutional societies were united in the National Union of Women's Suffrage Societies, led by Millicent Garrett Fawcett. She was married to a radical politician and had been in the fray, fighting for women's votes, since the 1860s. She knew that the struggle would be long and hard. As the writer Mary Stott, born in 1907, says of her:

She kept on, without faltering, for sixty years. All through my life when things have been tough, when I've worked on various campaigns and it's taken so long and we don't seem to be getting anywhere, I've said to myself, Remember MGF. Knowing she did it is a source of strength. It keeps you going.

Quoted in Dale Spender,
There's Always Been
A Women's Movement
This Century,
Pandora Press, 1983

Millicent Fawcett saw that men would have to vote in Parliament to give women the vote and that they would not do so until they could be persuaded that this was in their own interest. Women were in a 'Catch 22' situation. They were denied political experience, access to serious discussion and power, and then discounted because they had no political experience, serious discussion or power. 'If we had votes,' she is quoted as saying, 'it would be easy to get votes.' Opponents – mainly men – thought her 'advanced' and 'unsexing' when she spoke at public meetings. After she and another suffragist had advocated votes for women from a public platform, an MP told the House of Commons of 'two ladies, wives of members of this House, who had disgraced themselves'. Millicent Fawcett praised the suffragettes in 1906 for 'doing more to bring the movement within the region of practical politics in twelve months, than I and my followers have been able to do in the same number of years'. But she did not condone violence:

Sylvia Pankhurst,
London, 1912
photo: BBC Hulton

17

The fact that men under similar circumstances have been much more violent and destructive does not inspire us with the wish to imitate them.

Millicent Fawcett, 'Progress of the Women's Movement in the United Kingdom', in Ida Husted Harper (ed.), **History of Woman Suffrage**, National American Woman Suffrage Association, 1922

The democratic machinery of the suffragists was efficient and their organization exemplary. Their by-election policy, membership fees, basis of representation, devolution into federations, were planned and organized so as to be capable of indefinite expansion. They published a newspaper called the **Common Cause**. Official campaign organizers arranged meetings, collected money, sold newspapers. The suffragists dared to have a public face at a time when women were consigned to service and to private life. They appealed to reasonableness in men and enterprise in women. Local societies grew, and by 1910 the NUWSS was powerful nationwide.

The militant society was entirely different. They were impatient with the lack of progress of the law-abiding suffragists. From 1906 on, they provided the impetus for a new strategy. Their motto was 'Deeds not Words'. While the suffragists organized the bureaucracy for change, the suffragettes supplied the theatre, the publicity and the innovatory tactics. They were out to make a fuss. They wanted their public protest to be newsworthy and this they achieved. The women's movement of subsequent years, in particular the Greenham women, drew on both strategies – organization, but theatre too.

Women's Social and Political Union Shop
photo: BBC Hulton

Tactics for Change

The Women's Social and Political Union was formed in Manchester in 1905 by Emmeline Pankhurst and her daughters, Sylvia and Christabel. Mrs Pankhurst's feminist views were sharpened by her work on the Board of Poor Law Guardians and then as a Registrar of Births and Deaths in a working-class district. Of the men working on the Board she said:

I found that the law was being very harshly administered . . . They were guardians not of the poor, but of the rates and as I soon discovered, not very astute guardians even of money.

From
Midge Mackenzie,
**Shoulder to Shoulder:
A Documentary**,
Penguin, 1975

As a registrar she was shocked by the conditions of many women's existence:

I have had little girls of thirteen come to my office to register the birth of their babies, illegitimate of course. In many of the cases I found that the child's own father or some near relative was responsible for her state. There was nothing that could be done in most cases . . . During my term of office a very young mother of an illegitimate child exposed her baby and it died. The girl was tried for murder and sentenced to death. This was afterwards commuted it is true but . . . from the point of view of justice, the real murderer of the baby received no punishment at all.

Arrest of Mrs Pankhurst, 1908
photo: BBC Hulton

She saw that women as a group were powerless, exploited and disregarded:

> It was rapidly becoming clear to my mind that men regarded women as a servant class in the community and that women were going to remain in that servant class until they lifted themselves out of it. I asked myself many times . . . what was to be done.

What was to be done was for women to get the vote. By February 1907 the WSPU had 47 branches. By May there were 58; by August there were 70. And money poured in as fast as members:

> Women everywhere were practising 'self-denial' to give money to the cause. The more acts of militancy, the more rolled in. The income rose with increasing momentum, reaching £3,000 in 1906–7, £7,000 in 1907–8, £20,000 in 1908–9, £32,000 in 1909–10. Every other organization in the country wondered at the income of the WSPU.

Sylvia Pankhurst,
The Suffragette Movement,
Longmans, 1931;
Virago, 1977

According to Ray Strachey, historian of the women's movement at that time, the WSPU did not spend as much time on the formalities of organization as the NUWSS. Decisions were made by the Pankhursts and by the Treasurer, Mrs Pethick-Lawrence. No record was kept of who joined and no regular subscriptions were paid. Money came in fast, but it went out faster on flags, banners, leaflets, meetings, parades, shows, drums and even bombs. Anything to make a noise and stir. Perhaps unsurprisingly in such a volatile movement, differences of opinion broke out and separate societies were formed – such as the Women's Freedom League in 1909. But whatever the tactics adopted by the different organizations, all saw getting the vote as the key to changing man-made laws and reforming the restrictions and injustices of women's lives.

The militants heckled Cabinet ministers at meetings, sent deputations to ministers at the House of Commons – who refused to see them – and got arrested for obstruction. They chained themselves to the railings at Downing Street and made eloquent speeches before being hauled off to Bow Street. One was found chained to a statue in the House of Commons. Another was found hiding in an organ loft. Repeatedly they tried to see the Prime Minister, Asquith. Repeatedly he refused to see them. Their protests in the early years were orderly. Small deputations of women filed towards Westminster. Cordons of police met them on foot and horse-back. The police would order the women back. The women would refuse. Scuffles and convictions for obstruction usually followed and they would be sent to Holloway prison.

Generalities about the nature of the female sex – their hysteria, lack of reason, emotionalism – filled leading articles in newspapers. The suffragettes moved from passive to active militancy. In prison they claimed the status of political prisoners. They made accusations and revelations about the prison routine which embarrassed the authorities. They refused to eat. They fought against being forcibly fed. As soon as they got ill from inanition, the prison authorities released them. They

Parade of Suffragettes outside Parliament, 1912
photo: BBC Hulton

did not want corpses on their hands. Holloway hadn't been designed to house these upper-class women in their black silk gowns and elastic-sided boots alive, let alone dead.

The Conciliation Bill

Private Members' Bills advocating votes for women were introduced in 1907 and 1908, but got nowhere. Then in 1910 there was a General Election. The Liberal government was re-elected but an all-party committee known as a Conciliation Committee drafted a Bill on women's suffrage. The WSPU called a truce to militancy to give the Bill a chance. For six months there was unparalleled intensity of propaganda – marches, processions, meetings. Twice in a week the Albert Hall was packed. Asquith deigned to receive a deputation from the constitutional societies. Dublin sent its Mayor and public officials in their robes of state to appeal to the House of Commons. The councils of 129 important towns, including Edinburgh, Glasgow, Liverpool, Birmingham and Newcastle, declared their official support. The Conciliation Bill was put to the House of Commons in July 1910. **The Times** published articles against it every day for the preceding fortnight, despite which it passed its second reading by 110 votes. But the power of patriarchy won the day. Ministers such as Lloyd George and Winston Churchill attacked the Bill as undemocratic and it was killed.

In its place a Reform Bill destined to extend suffrage for men was put on the Liberal programme. This, it was made clear, might or might not be amended to include women. Since the 1800s the male electorate had increased from 700,000 to seven million, but nothing was in sight for women:

If it had been the Prime Minister's object to enrage every woman suffragist to the point of frenzy, he could not have acted with greater perspicacity.

Millicent Fawcett,
quoted in Ray Strachey,
The Cause,
G. Bell, 1928; Virago, 1978

23

Suffrage work went on. The National Union added 60 new branches in 1910. There was a Men's League for Women's Suffrage, the Actresses' Suffrage League, the Artists' Suffrage League, the Catholic Women's Suffrage Society, the Church League for Women's Suffrage, the Conservative and Unionist Women's Franchise Association, the Free Church League and the Friends' League, the Jewish League, the London Graduates' League, the Scottish Universities Women's Suffrage Union, and so on.

The WSPU were less philosophical and followed a different course. They smashed windows, poured acid into post boxes, cut telephone wires, set fire to empty houses, destroyed golf courses and threw bombs at churches. Their destructive acts were all directed at property, not people. None the less their behaviour confirmed in their enemies' minds that women were too depraved ever to be granted the responsibility of the right to vote. Christabel Pankhurst put the militant case in a leaflet for the WSPU:

> It is only simple justice that women demand. They have worked for their political enfranchisement as men never worked for it, by a constitutional agitation carried on on a far greater scale than any franchise agitation in the past. For fifty years they have been striving and have met with nothing but trickery and betrayal at the hands of politicians. Cabinet Ministers have taunted them with their reluctance to use the violent methods that were being used by men before they won the extension of the franchise in 1829, in 1832 and in 1867. They have used women's dislike of violence as a

**Militant suffragettes
burn a church, 1913**
photo: Topham

reason for withholding from them the rights of citizenship . . . The message of the broken pane is that women are determined that the lives of their sisters shall no longer be broken, and that in future those who have to obey the law shall have a voice in saying what the law shall be. Repression cannot break the spirit of liberty.

'Broken Windows',
WSPU leaflet 88,
The Woman's Press, 1912

The Reform Bill could have been tailored to give all adults suffrage, or to give the vote to married women over 25, or to give the vote to women who were householders. In 1913 the Speaker of the House of Commons said that in his opinion the adoption of any of the women's suffrage amendments would so alter the Bill as to make it no longer the same Bill, and that consequently it would have to be killed if any such amendments were adopted. None were.

Trouble followed this bitter blow. An attempt was made in 1913 to burn down Lloyd George's country house. Emmeline Pankhurst was found guilty and sentenced to three years for 'inciting to commit a felony'. On previous occasions she had gone on hunger strike and quickly been released, but the government was now out to punish these women who were causing them such embarrassment. It introduced what became known as the 'Cat and Mouse Act', aimed solely at suffragettes. If they got dangerously weak on hunger strike they were released, then reimprisoned without a further trial as soon as they regained their strength. Despite this dubious legislation, a year after her arrest in 1913 Mrs Pankhurst had contrived to spend only 30 days in prison. She had gone on hunger strike twelve times.

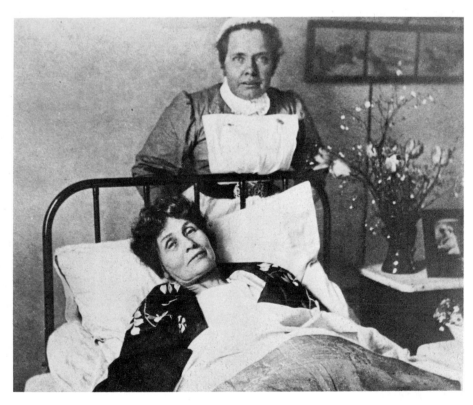

Mrs Pankhurst on hunger strike
photo: Museum of London

The funeral of the suffragette Emily Davison, who threw herself under the King's horse, Derby Day 1913 photo: PP & M It

On Derby Day 1913, the suffragette Emily Davison flung herself under the king's horse and was killed. People read accounts of this dramatic suicide in newspapers all over the world. It became known that in Britain there were women who would die for the conviction that women should be free. A huge procession of women dressed in white wound through the London streets on the way to her funeral. Emily Davison had honours degrees in English, classics and mathematics and had worked as a journalist and teacher:

Emily Davison's death, 1913
photo: BBC Hulton

> She led a very ordinary life for a woman of her type and times. She was imprisoned eight times; she was forcibly fed forty-nine times. That is the kind of life to which we dedicate our best and kindest and wittiest women . . . if when we walked behind her bier on Saturday we thought of ourselves doing a dead comrade honour, we were wrong. We were making a march of penitence behind a victim we allowed the Government to do to death.

Mrs Pankhurst, out of prison under the Cat and Mouse Act, tried to attend the funeral, but was arrested.

> Mrs Pankhurst was very ill, so ill that her nurse had tried to dissuade her from rising for the funeral lest she should die on the way. And now she was taken back to Holloway and the hunger strike. I felt a feeling that is worse than grief.

Rebecca West,
Clarion,
20 June 1913

One hundred and eighty-two other suffragettes were also in prison. The drama and intensity of the struggle meant that the 'women issue' was never out of the news.

For their part the suffragists held incessant public meetings. Their membership doubled in 1913. Forty thousand 'friends of women's suffrage' were enrolled. In June of that year the suffragists organized a huge pilgrimage. Women set out on foot from all parts of the country and converged on London. At every town and village they spoke on the suffrage issue and more joined the march. On 26 July they reached Hyde Park and held a massive rally.

Still the government made no move. The political impasse remained. The only hope of progress appeared to lie in a change of government. Women went on campaigning. The police became increasingly heavy-handed. The involvement of working-class women grew; in 1914 Sylvia Pankhurst led marches of the East London Federation of Suffragettes, which was entirely composed of poor working-class women.

The Wages of War

Then came the war. Suffrage activities stopped, militancy faded and no more was heard of the WSPU. Some thought it a betrayal to abandon 'the cause' for what they regarded as male warmongering, but such sentiments were scorned in the jingoism of the hour. 'Your country needs you' was the slogan now. Men were sent to fight and die in the muddy trenches of Belgium and France, and women were used as a vast reserve labour force to make the shells and bombs required /

to do the killing. High explosives were what was needed. Roles were polarized. Men were to be heroes and behind every hero is a good woman. 'Without women victory will tarry,' said Lloyd George. 'And the victory which tarries means a victory whose footprints are footprints of blood.' Ninety per cent of women did work customarily done by men, but no assurances were forthcoming about equal pay: 'They will be unskilled and untrained and cannot quite turn out as much work as men can who have been at it for some time.'

By the end of the war one and a half million more women were working than in 1914. Newspapers were eloquent and gave praise where previously they had slandered. 'The nation is grateful to the women,' they said, not accepting that women *were* the nation just as much as men. When the nurse Edith Cavell was shot in 1915 for hiding British soldiers in Germany, Asquith said in tribute: 'There are thousands of such women, but a year ago we did not know it.' Men of all kinds formed a wider judgement of women. It was not quite logical to be converted to the idea of women's suffrage because a woman who had been a good milliner could also be a good munitions worker, but that's how it was.

As for the vexed question of suffrage . . . The shenanigans behind the allocating of votes to women displayed the cynicism of the political world. The war made the existing register of voters a farce. Not one man in five was at the place where he had registered when the lists were made. Nor were men sufficiently stationary to be registered anew. When the war ended there would be an election. A new register was needed. In 1916 a group of MPs began to press for a register based on war service. The National Union of Women's Suffrage Societies responded smartly. They wrote to the Prime Minister pointing out that women too were doing war work. They said they could not allow an alteration in the basis of voting for men without consideration of their claims too. They continued campaigning. They sent deputations to their MPs. Public opinion was behind them. 'In the past we have opposed the claim . . . we were wrong,' wrote the **Observer** on 13 August 1916. Even Asquith seemed to mellow. 'It is true that women cannot fight in the sense of going out with rifles and so forth . . . but they have aided in the most effective way in the prosecution of the war.' Women who 'held the fort' for soldiers, on lower wages and without any job security, might earn the right to vote. Women who were militant in their demands for that right on the grounds of equality of citizenship, ability, intellect and oppor-tunity were punished as lawbreakers and treated with scorn.

Lloyd George became Prime Minister in 1917. An all-party com-mittee was assigned the task of drafting 'proposals on the franchise and registration difficulty'. They recommended 33 franchise reforms, including a clause which, if adopted, would give married women over 30 the right to vote. That would enfranchise six of the eleven million adult women.

The committee's recommendations were put to Parliament as the Representation of the People Bill. To make sure it got through, women war workers organized a huge demonstration with representative women from 70 differ-ent trades – lamplighters, engine cleaners, postwomen, nurses, lacemakers. They kept the issue in the public eye. In the House of Commons MPs spoke of ruin to the State and disaster to the Home, but the Bill was carried, with the contentious clause, by 329 votes to 40. In the House of Lords 134 peers voted for the women's suffrage clause, 71 voted against and 13 abstained. The Bill had survived both Houses and on 6 February 1918 it got the Royal Assent and became law.

In Millicent Fawcett's view, no doubt correct, there was little commitment to social justice for women behind the passing of the Bill. The government, forced by the circumstances of war to compile a new register for men, could not continue to justify the total exclusion of women from it:

> I do not believe we should have won the vote just when we did, except for the fact that it was absolutely necessary to introduce legislation in order to prevent the almost total disfranchisement of many millions of men who had been serving their country abroad in the Navy and Army, or in munition or other work which had withdrawn them from places where they usually resided . . . The most important qualification for the Parliamentary franchise, before 1918, was the occupation of premises, and before a man could be put on a register of voters it was necessary for its owner to prove 'occupation' of these premises for twelve months previous to the last 15th of July. Millions of the best men in the country had become disqualified through their war service by giving up their qualifying premises. Therefore by sheer necessity the Government was forced to introduce legislation dealing with the whole franchise question as it affected the male voter . . . An age limit of thirty was imposed upon women, not because it was in any way logical or reasonable, but simply and solely to produce a constituency in which the men were not outnumbered by the women.

Millicent Fawcett, 'Progress of the Women's Movement in the United Kingdom', in Ida Husted Harper (ed.), **History of Woman Suffrage**, 1922

It was after such cynical considerations that some women gained their rights.

Women over 30 get the vote, 1918
photo: BBC Hulton

When the war ended in 1918 women workers were dismissed by thousands from one day to the next. There were protests. Twenty thousand women, paid off at Woolwich Arsenal, marched to Whitehall and demanded to see Lloyd George. But it had been made clear by government and unions that women war workers were only 'filling in' and that the jobs belonged to those soldiers who returned alive. Working conditions went back to their pre-war shape. It was expedient again to imply that women had no business to be in factories at all. Their proper place was in the home. It is a recurrent view, given official sanction again in the 1980s when jobs have been made scarce. A million women went back to their homes and their unpaid labour there. One in three women had to be self-supporting. For them, home was what they made of it. Over 750,000 young men had been killed in the fighting. Marriage was no longer automatically a woman's fate. Many women endured severe and protracted unemployment on a dole that was less than for men. Those who stayed in work suffered wage-cutting of their already lower rates during the slump. Women's labour failed to get a footing.

Even so, the years which immediately followed partial franchise brought a harvest of gains for women. In 1920 the Sex Disqualification Removal Act opened the legal profession and accountancy to women. In 1922 Lady Astor became the first woman MP. The same year women were admitted to Oxford University and to the Civil Service, and the Law of Property Act made wives, mothers and daughters equal to husbands, fathers and sons in cases of intestacy. In 1923 the Matrimonial Causes Act made the grounds of divorce the same for women and men. And then, in 1928, Stanley Baldwin and the Conservative government lifted the insulting age discrimination and gave women the vote on the same basis as men. Baldwin pronounced:

The subjection of women if there be such a thing, will not now depend on any creation of the law, nor can it be remedied by any action of the law. It will never again be possible to blame the sovereign state for any position of inequality. Women will have with us the fullest rights. The ground and justification for the old agitation is gone for ever.

Perhaps he knew that was rhetoric. Sixty years on the 'old agitation' is still there. To have the legislation is not at all the same thing as to have the state of affairs that the legislation claims to achieve. It is easier to fight for tangible objectives, such as the vote, than to fight to eradicate the prejudice underpinning the denial. There is danger of 'tokenism' in any equality legislation if the society implementing it has no real commitment to equality.

But feminists of subsequent years learned valuable lessons from the suffragists and the suffragettes. They observed their courage, tenacity and defiance and were inspired by it. They observed that in order to achieve their objectives they must organize and go on fighting regardless of setback or disappointment. And they observed that any spirit of egalitarianism in men does not automatically extend to women when it comes to position, pay and power.

**Women get the vote
on the same basis as men, 1928**
photo: Museum of Labour History

Crane-workers in a shell factory, 1914–18   photo: Imperial War Museum

2. 'FLINT AND ROSES. VERY ODD': WOMEN'S WORK IN WARTIME.

Coal heaver, 1914
photo: Imperial War Museum

In the two world wars of 1914 and 1939 women 'manned' the factories while men were sent to fight. Women were used by government as a reserve labour force. The experience was useful in subsequent years in women's struggle for equality of opportunity. It showed that the passive, domestic identity imposed on them historically was a fabrication. They could as well be stokers, welders and crane-drivers as needleworkers. And it showed that governments unprepared to grant women equal rights of citizenship, status, pay or opportunity were perfectly prepared to exploit their capacity for equality of work performance if it was expedient so to do.

Before the First World War, notions of feminine identity were narrow. A host of prescriptive publications cropped up in the nineteenth century – mostly written by women – with titles like **The English Maiden**, **The Feminine Soul**, **Woman, Her Social and Domestic Character**, **The Afternoon of Unmarried Life**, and there was a whole series on Women, Wives, Mothers and Daughters of England. These manuals of behaviour harped on self-effacement, repression, patience, resignation, appearance and a trivial round of domestic duties. Men were considered superior – mentally, physically and morally. Education would be wasted on women, responsibility would overwhelm them and work would make them ill. Upper-class women must be sheltered, protected and indulged. Skivvies must serve with a smile. All had credible status only in so far as they were the wives, mothers or daughters of men. An unmarried woman was superfluous – a spinster, an old maid, someone's maiden aunt – unless she had money, which was seldom the case:

> A single woman with a narrow income must be a ridiculous old maid, the proper sport of boys and girls: but a single woman of good fortune is always respectable and may be as sensible and pleasant as anybody else.

Jane Austen, **Emma**

Marriage and motherhood were considered to be every woman's true preoccupation. The virtues and skills which it was right and proper to cultivate were those which would be useful in these capacities. Some men might want good cooking and wholesome stupidity, some might want intelligent and glamorous companionship, but ambition, achievement, independence and success were unfeminine and likely to have as their threatened price social and sexual ostracism. Obedience, humility, reticence and unselfishness were the true reflections of the feminine soul:

In the case of a highly gifted woman, nothing can be more injudicious or fatal to her happiness than an exhibition of the least disposition to presume upon such gifts. Let a husband be once subjected to a feeling of jealousy which, without the strictest watchfulness will be liable to arise, and her peace of mind and her free agency are alike destroyed for the rest of her life; or at any rate, until she can convince him afresh, by a long continuance of the most scrupulous conduct, that the injury committed against him was purely accidental and foreign alike to her feelings and her inclinations.

Mrs Ellis,
'Behaviour to Husbands',
in **Women of England,
Their Social Duties and
Domestic Habits**, 1839

There were plenty of dissenters from these networks of fallacy, and a few determined enough, if those were the terms, to give the whole idea of marriage a miss: 'I have a mind,' wrote Florence Nightingale as she declined her suitor, 'an active nature which requires satisfaction and would not find it in his life.' The suffragist Millicent Fawcett described her humiliation when a man who had stolen her purse was accused of the theft of the property of Professor Henry Fawcett. Women authors got published by using male pseudonyms. There was organized agitation by women for reforms to the laws affecting their property rights, education, divorce, custody of children and working conditions. And of course there was the focus on the denial of franchise.

Among the largest class, the faceless class, the working class, women beavered away as hard as men, but for less reward. However unladylike its nature, hard work was their lot. If they went out to work their rates of pay were pitifully low and if they didn't go out to work there were no rates of pay at all. They worked as servants, cleaners, parlour maids, laundry maids, dressmakers, milliners, governesses, in the cotton mills, in shops and hotel service and luxury goods manufacture. In the dressmaking profession girls and women would work 15 hours a day, often in dark and overcrowded rooms. They were given little money and miserable lodgings. Some women's jobs were heavy, some light, some skilled, some simple. The common factor of them all was that they were badly paid.

Despite the hard grind of most women's lives it was the image of femininity propounded by the little books of moral maxims that held the greatest sway: 'A grown-up daughter ought to nurse her mother if she is ill, or teach her little brother to read.' And when she could see nothing 'at once important and undoubted to do', she was 'to dress as well as she can and to play on the pianoforte'. Fear of being 'unladylike' or 'unmaidenly' was acute. Its price was no kisses, no husband, no money, no home. Women were and must be guardians of the hearth and home-makers. Family life was their domain. And upper-class mothers and daughters for the most part concurred with this description as men concurred with an expected image of being aggressive, chivalrous, strong and clever.

The First World War

In 1914 war came. Notions of femininity were blown sky-high. Ladies and maidens became decidedly butch. Everyone knew that men were warriors. Few knew that women were stokers, foundry workers and machine-gun manufacturers. It was equivalent to telling men to wear skirts and do tatting. Suddenly

**Shovelling hops
into a kiln, 1914–18**
photo: Imperial War Museum

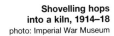

35

women were to be androgynous. They were to wear men's clothes, scrape back their hair and do rough work. It wasn't an extension of identity that they discovered for themselves, but one imposed on them through political expediency. Suddenly women's 'natural' role was discovered to be not so vital after all:

. . . women who had never known industrial life, women from the counter, the desk, the domestic hearth, or the quietude of an artist's life, put down all these less essential tasks to take their place in the munition factories. Undismayed by the difficulties of an unfamiliar task, undaunted by the obstacles necessarily attending a huge reorganization of industry, these women have mastered their job and from the simpler operations in the engineering shop have steadily advanced to the more expert processes. They have developed into the most able of tool-setters and guagers, or testers of completed work; they are efficient operators in the manufacture of machine guns and in the production of high explosives and aeroplanes, and they can successfully manipulate the making and assembling of a fuse, the latter process being comparable in delicacy with the art of watch-making. Not only have women undertaken such operations where fineness of touch and nicety of judgment are the essential qualifications – many are now 'turning' shells accurately up to one-five-thousandth part of an inch, a feat formerly considered almost impossible to a man – but they have been found competent workers in the shipyards and in the foundries. In the ship-building yards women are employed with success as red-leaders, rough painters, carpenters and electric wire layers on board H. M. ships. In one

36

Red Cross nurses, 1915
photo: Beaford Archive

factory, a woman smith is now employed with satisfactory results, and in a foundry, where the work is mainly on turbine and steam cylinder castings, a woman stoker is at present giving great satisfaction.

In all these varied occupations and multitudinous processes women in the munition factories have proved themselves not only efficient workers, but in some cases superior to their men fellow-workers . . . not only has the efficiency of the woman munition-maker been proved, but ample demonstration has been given that her physical endurance and *morale* is comparable to that of her men-folk in the trenches, and one might say with justice of the average woman-worker in the munition factories that:

> 'You never hear her do a growl or whine;
> She's made of flint and roses, very odd.'

Indeed, these women, now numbering some 700,000, who are working at the production of munitions by day and by night, at the cost of personal sacrifice, have in the satisfaction of their own conscience, earned the admiration of the whole nation.

Behind the eulogy was a smack of cynicism. Women were now lauded for doing dirty work for which they would have been vilified in peacetime. There is the usual assumption that the nation is men rather than women too – the campaigns for suffrage and equal rights are ignored – and the flattery ends abruptly with a direct recruitment call that showed women up for what they were – a reservoir of surplus labour:

37

Tarring the roads, 1914–18
photo: Imperial War Museum

. . . every possible fit man must be released to serve with the Forces, and gaps in the essential war industries, such as munition making, must be filled from other sources. The nation looks with confidence to the women of Great Britain to fill these gaps. It, therefore, behoves every woman who is physically fit and between the ages of 18 and 40 years, who is not already engaged in productive work, to offer her services to her country. The munition factory provides an open road to present duty and a convenient recruiting station can be found at any Employment Exchange, or at one of the 39 Training Schools for munition workers, which have been established in London and at various provincial Centres by the Ministry of Munitions, in conjunction with the local Education Authorities.

L. Keyser Yates,
Women's Work in War Time, 1917

There is a unique collection of documents and photographs in the Imperial War Museum library in London, assembled by a women's war work sub-committee which contacted every individual and association involved with women's work in the 1914–18 war. The collection, which fills more than 200 box-files, shows that women did every conceivable kind of work. Men poured out of the vital services and industries and into the army. Women were called and they came 'for the duration'. Some came from occupations put out of business by the war. Women previously 'unoccupied', in the Census use of the term, went to work. They came from all classes and were of all ages and types. A large proportion of them were married.

Industrial Britain became a huge arsenal. Munitions were wanted on a vast and unanticipated scale. At the outset of the war there were three

Fire-fighters, 1914–18
photo: BBC Hulton

national munitions factories. As the conflict went on, 5,000 privately run but government-controlled munitions factories were set up. Ninety per cent of women working in these factories did work customarily done by men. Shell-making was the most important single trade. Women often worked seven days a week and 12 to 14 hours a day without proper safety precautions. Those working with TNT were jocularly called 'canaries' – poisoning made their skin turn yellow. The journal of the medical profession blamed the victims:

Often neglect on the part of the workers to follow simple precautions leads to disturbance of health. They are offered authoritative help but refuse to help themselves. The observance of regulations can be made with little inconvenience and be still consistent with maximum output of munitions.

Lancet,
12 August 1916

Women worked in all types of occupations, including many previously barred to them. There was no conscription, but government pressure was strong. A string of publications offered them jobs:

Agriculture. Hours of work 10–12 a day. 3–4 weeks training on farms. Pay, 18 shillings a week. Intending workers should be at least 18, active, intelligent, physically strong and prepared to sign on for the duration of the war.

They were urged to work as ambulance drivers, bus conductors, canteen workers and carpenters 'for army hut construction at home and in France', as clerks and secretaries, club leaders and commercial travellers, as crèche matrons,

dental mechanics and doctors (there were 1,100 women doctors on the medical register), as gardeners, lamplighters, mail van drivers, motor drivers, patrol workers 'with a view to controlling and restraining the girlhood of the country at a time when such influence is urgently needed', as pharmacists, policewomen in munitions factories – searching for contraband matches and the like – sanitary inspectors, taxi drivers, teachers, tram conductors, as well as in the armed services and in scores of voluntary jobs.

The number of women in commercial jobs rose from 500,000 to one million, in the professions from 50,000 to 120,000, in transport from 18,000 to 115,000, in the Civil Service from 66,000 to 225,000, in industry from two million to three million. Nor did they stop being mothers, though wifehood was in abeyance for a while. Working men had 'home comforts' provided by women. Working women had double roles.

'For the Duration'

In virtually every woman's contract of employment, the phrase 'for the duration' appeared. The understanding was that women would quit when the war was over and return to less skilled and less visible pursuits. Agreements between government and unions stipulated that come peacetime jobs would revert to their previous holders. And though public admiration of women's contribution was freely and lyrically expressed, it did not translate itself into a desire, still less a determination, to see that they got pay parity. Women's presumed inferiority was useful when it came to paying them less than men. Managers complained that girls were being paid more than they were worth. Newspapers dubbed equality claims as unpatriotic. Those men who, perhaps understandably, did not want to find themselves in the army saw women's work capability as a threat to their jobs. The government was openly opposed to equal pay for women. The unions were vague and equivocal. Employers were told to take on women 'provided this shall not affect adversely the rate customarily paid for the job'. This was loose enough to be interpreted to suit the employer's purse. The 'rate' could be taken to mean the piece rate, not the time rate, and readjusting machinery and processes was a way of ensuring that former piece rates no longer applied. One way or another it was arranged that women were paid less than men for doing identical work and less for identical amounts of work on systems of payment by result.

Nevertheless women did earn more than they had before, though in real terms their earnings did little more than keep up with the rise in the cost of living. Their average wage in 1914 was 13s. 6d. a week, and by 1918 this had gone up to 35s, but the cost of living had doubled too. They were, however, earning two thirds as much as men by the end of the war – the same ratio as now – compared to less than half in 1914. This was a direct result of their entry into what had been men's jobs. In traditional 'women's work' – dressmaking, millinery, laundering – wages stayed down, unaffected by war conditions.

Where women did achieve improvements in pay and conditions,

it was because they organized. The National Federation of Women Workers fought for the 'munition girls' with the slogan 'equal pay for equal work'. In 1915 the Women's Trade Union League got a deal, giving all 'substituted' women a minimum wage of £1 a week. They achieved agreements on overtime and holiday pay, and government acceptance of the principle that skilled women should be paid the same as skilled men. The government honoured the deals, but not the private firms. And everywhere the minimum rate tended to stay the maximum. On the railways 'substituted' women got the minimum time rates, but there were huge discrepancies in the bonus rates. Women shop assistants got four fifths of the men's rate. Private employers were openly discriminatory over women's earnings. Arbitration took months and awards were not back-dated. None the less the Federation won 90 per cent of its arbitration cases and the war years saw the strengthening of women's trade-union involvement. By 1918 there were 28 women delegates to the Trades Union Congress out of a total of 881. Eight of these women were from the Federation.

Had they not organized, women would have fared much worse than they did. And not only women. Their efforts also benefited the men who were to survive the war and return to their jobs. It was in their interests too that rates should be fixed at a living, not a sweated level. In 1918 the demobilization of women war workers was as fast as that of men from the army. War work ended, industry contracted and the soldiers were home. The jobs were theirs. Employers would have liked to keep women on in all manner of jobs – they wanted the cheap labour – but that was not allowed. If women opposed dismissal they were called parasites and blacklegs where before they had been hailed as heroines and saviours. Whatever they might have wanted in terms of economic and social independence was irrelevant. But it was also impossible to put the clock back. The war had enormously increased the number of 'surplus' women. One in every three now had to be self-supporting. It had broken up innumerable homes and created a class of 'new poor'. Prices had doubled since 1914, so women dependent on small allowances or fixed incomes could no longer manage. Census figures for 1921 showed 9,516,753 women 'unoccupied' and 4,209,408 in the labour market.

In the post-war years women were excluded from most jobs, the dole for them was lower than for men, the domestic context was shattered for many, and the country was plunging into economic depression. But women had discovered the useful weapon of a double identity. The Angel in the House was also Rosie the Riveter. 'Flint and Roses. Very Odd.' Women began to appear more free. They got the vote and education and divorce reforms and the right at least to become lawyers and MPs. Skirts got shorter and so did hair. Women smoked cigarettes and played hockey, and those that could afford it drove motor cars. Labour-saving devices made housework easier. And in the villages the Women's Institutes, which had begun during the war years as part of the national effort, developed in peacetime, bringing instruction and variety and breaking down class distinctions. Women were 'coming out' in all manner of ways. What they were prevented from coming into, as ever, was the power and the pay.

Unemployment march, Derby to London, 1934
photo: Museum of London

Seeing the soldiers off to war, 1940
photo: BBC Hulton

The Second World War

When the Second World War came, women again flooded into the labour force. This time, though, they went to work not simply because of moral and financial pressure – they were 'called up'. Recruitment was done by the Ministry of Labour and National Service. 'Essential work orders' were issued which ensured that women got their jobs and training through local Ministry offices. They were again combed out from 'less essential' peacetime jobs like domestic labour, sewing, clerical, shop and factory work. By 1944, 90 per cent of single women aged 18 to 40, 80 per cent of single women aged 40 to 59, and 81 per cent of married women and widows with no young children, were working in industry, civil defence and the forces. Their average weekly earnings increased by between 60 and 90 per cent. There was a short-lived emancipation of working women that 40 subsequent years of peacetime campaigning failed to achieve.

'There is a job awaiting every woman. The Army in the Factory must keep the Army in the Field supplied with the right equipment at the right time.' That was the call to arms in **Munitions Girl: A Handbook for the Women of the Industrial Army.** It gave details and syllabuses of government training schemes in sheet-metal work, panel-beating, oxy-acetylene welding, instrument-making, electrical installation, motor mechanics and dozens of other unladylike jobs. Women drove three-ton lorries. They 'manned' the aircraft factories. They became highly skilled tank-engine makers. Firms sceptical of employing women were again compelled by necessity to do so. Erstwhile housewives built concrete mixers. They worked as welders, fitters, plumbers, drillers, machine operators, shapers, bricklayers, braziers, labourers, boilersmiths, crane operators, train drivers, control operators, painters. They worked in the heavy chemical industry, they shovelled coal, they operated cement mixers. They did repetitive precision work such as drilling and riveting. They loaded railway trucks, they worked in the smiths' shops and foundries. Often they worked a sixty-hour week. They were transferred from one area to another to meet the needs of war production. Women with children were exempted from mobilization regulations, but many took jobs of their own accord, or joined some branch of the voluntary services.

The armed forces absorbed far more women than in the First World War. In the Women's Auxiliary Air Force (WAAF) they worked as radio operators, signallers, plotters and photographers. They test-flew aircraft and operated barrage balloons. They formed one tenth of the air transport auxiliary, ferrying aircraft from factories to air fields and transporting blood banks to hospitals. In the Women's Royal Naval Service (WRNS) they were instructors and meteorologists, they tested and repaired torpedoes and depth charges. They did clerical, communications, technical and signals work. In the Auxiliary Territorial Service they worked as motor drivers, cooks, orderlies and storewomen, teleprinter operators, kine-theodolite operators, despatch riders and draughtswomen. They did gunnery research and anti-aircraft duties.

To maintain agriculture the Women's Land Army was founded.

Early in the war farmers were reluctant to employ women: 17,000 volunteers enrolled, but only 5,000 were placed. By 1943, however, there were not enough recruits to go round. They did every type of farmwork – driving tractors, ploughing, draining, fruit spraying, forestry work. Their pay doubled, but was still about half that for men.

In the Home Guard women were clerks, telephonists, cooks and drivers. In the Women's Voluntary Service they looked after emergency feeding and clothing, evacuation of children and billeting of soldiers. In the Women's Home Defence organization they learned musketry, signalling, ju-jitsu and how to use grenades and bombs. And of course at home they did all the usual things like the sewing and the laundry and cooking on scarce rations. What they didn't do was to drop the bombs and fire the guns.

When it came to job security there was a distinct sense of *déjà vu*. The National Service Armed Forces Act provided rights of reinstatement for men when they came back from the war. The various employers' federations and trade unions agreed that women be regarded as temporarily employed. It was the familiar story of women holding the fort for the real workers.

As for pay . . . The 'Wages' chapter in the **Munitions Girl** handbook makes wry reading. The author was Caroline Haslett, President of the Women's Engineering Society and adviser to the Ministry of Labour and National Service on women's training throughout the war. 'This chapter provides more difficulty than any other in the book,' she wrote. Union agreements stipulated that women replacing men should be paid the 'man's rate' after six months. Nothing was mentioned about the wages of women who went on doing 'women's work'. Employers again altered 'men's jobs' before women took them over to avoid paying them fairly. Haslett admitted that in some places women were paid less than half as much as men for equivalent work. 'The best advice that can be given on the question of wages,' she wrote, 'is to discuss them with the shop steward.' Certainly women's trade-union representation doubled during the Second World War. A few unions, such as the Amalgamated Engineering Union, still did not accept women, but whereas in 1939 there were 970,000 women in trade unions, by 1943 there were 1,870,000 – 23 per cent of the total membership. And the principle of equal pay for equal work was at least established, even if it was not adhered to.

Making bombs, 1941
photo: BBC Hulton

In all manner of ways the seeds of a possible fairer deal for working women were sown during these years of social fracture. Works canteens were set up, freeing women from the necessity of always cooking an evening meal. Crèches and nurseries were organized for little children. A system of 'controlled absence' was devised for women with domestic responsibilities, who were allowed to take one shift a week off for shopping and domestic jobs. Part-time work for married women was encouraged by tax exemptions. There were home-working and outworking schemes. These are all social provisions of acute importance to women now as well as then.

The political and public presence of women led to a better deal for women during the war years. Women MPs – there were now 14 of them – were in the forefront. They formed the Women's Consultative Committee, which advised the govern-

**Painting the wings of
bomber planes, 1940–45**
photo: BBC Hulton

ment on 'the mobilizing of woman power'. They pressed for adequate state provision of day nurseries for the children of working mothers. They objected to the relegating of women with high qualifications to lowly jobs. They protested at women being used as cheap labour and pressed for better pay and welfare conditions and for women to be employed in their own districts. They objected to an all-male committee investigating welfare in the women's services and got a new committee elected of three men and five women. They pressed for all posts in the civil service and higher posts in government to be open to men and women equally. It was their idea to evacuate children without their mothers in groups supervised by teachers. They organized the distribution of rationed food, formed the Parliamentary Advisory Committee on Salvage and in many different ways were indispensable to the running of the country.

The influence of these MPs clearly showed the importance of representation by women for women at the decision-making level. In the 1945 General Election there were 87 women parliamentary candidates: 42 Labour, 20 Liberal, 13 Conservative and 12 others. Twenty-four were elected: 21 Labour, one Liberal, one Conservative and one Independent. It was the largest number of women MPs ever – only one less than there is today.

In 1946 a report was published by the International Labour Office called 'The War and Women's Employment: The Experience of the United Kingdom and the United States'. It ended by asking: 'Now that the war is over the following questions arise: what is to be the fate of women workers and what chances have they of consolidating and increasing under peacetime conditions the gains they won in emergency conditions?'

At a stroke women lost most of those gains. And their fate, as men took back 'their' jobs, was to be reclaimed by the badly paid 'women's jobs' where there was, and in some cases still is, an almost complete lack of trade-union organization – domestic and hotel work, clerical work, nursing, shop work. Or they went back full time to the serving side of family life – housework, cooking, shopping and so on.

A New Outlook
background to fashion media.
changes - hane
work.

It wasn't quite business as usual, however. Women benefited from the spirit of egalitarianism and reconstruction of the post-war years. The Women's Consultative Committee advised the government on 'questions relating to the resettlement of women in civilian life'. Women had acquired skills which they were unwilling simply to waste. They had received intensive and specialized training. Their horizons had widened and they had earned their own money. Government rehabilitation and vocational training courses were open to women and men who had worked in the war effort (but with different rates of allowances!). More women workers joined trade unions and efforts were made to safeguard women's interests in collective bargaining. The ban on married women teaching or working in the Civil Service was lifted. An act of 1942 recommended that all medical schools be open to women students and stipulated that grants to those schools be given only if they admitted a minimum of one in five women students. Sex barriers were lifted on all hospital appointments. Women were 'allowed in' to higher technical schools such as Faraday House Electrical Engineering College. Scholarships were made available to them for higher education in physics, chemistry, civil engineering, aeronautical construction, electrical engineering. School meals were provided and works canteens established to lighten the double task of married women workers with domestic responsibilities. A widespread system of kindergartens and day nurseries for two- to five-year-olds had been set up. Working hours were adjusted and part-time employment extended. 'A new psychological approach to the subject of women's work now exists,' said the report on 'The War and Women's Employment'. It went on:

back in
home
ads -
focus
on
home

It is this changed mental attitude that will contribute most to bringing the status of British women nearer to complete equality. Both in the armed forces and in the Civil Service highly responsible posts were held by women and the safety of countless lives depended on their ability and discretion in carrying out their duties. The general public is now quite accustomed to seeing important tasks entrusted to women.

But progress seemed concessive and partial while two crucial issues remained unfaced and unresolved: 'women's jobs' and 'men's jobs' – who should do them and why; and the matter of fair and equal pay. A Labour MP made a rare admission of masculine culpability:

Women have always asked two things. They have asked for opportunity and recognition and as far as opportunity is concerned it has largely come

Bricklayers, 1945
photo: Imperial War Museum

their way during the present war. When we come to recognition I confess that I do not think we have played quite fairly by them. We have had recognition in words. Recognition in words is very useful and flattering, but I do not think we have altogether had recognition in deeds, deeds meaning mainly remuneration. We have a standard in the Services that has been expressed roughly as a two-thirds standard – that a woman is worth financially about two thirds of a man. I do not think that standard can be maintained. I do not believe that that is in accordance with the views of the country and we have to do better than that. We have to put women as human beings on an equal footing with men in a great many ways in which we do not put them at the present time.

Confused signals were put out. Women had shown what they could do and been praised for it, but now they were denied the context to continue doing it. There was some recognition that equality of opportunity was desirable, but when it came to job allocation, it seemed that men must come first. They were historically the heads of households and the breadwinners and they were back from battle. The old spectre of **The Feminine Soul** and **Woman, Her Social and Domestic Character** floated back as an image of convenience. The final chapter of **Munitions Girl: A Handbook for the Women of the Industrial Army** exhorted:

Even if you are returning home to take up household duties, you will take with you a new tidiness and a new outlook. You will not be dependent on the 'mere male' to do repairs and you can put many of your own ideas on

50

The soldier's return, 1945
photo: BBC Hulton

house decoration into practice without waiting for a handyman. You will be ready to take your part in the new world of labour saving appliances and you will even be equipped to give an opinion on the design and manufacture of domestic equipment and to make the utmost use of it and to secure from it its full value.

F. W. Pethick-Lawrence, quoted in Margaret Goldsmith, **Women at War**, Lindsay Drummond, 1943

The Angel in the House could now fix the plumbing and tile the roof too. Not quite the stuff of equality.

Women had proved indispensable in the highly dubious scenario of war. They had shown their ability, their cooperation, their usefulness and their flexibility. They had shown that any job a man can do, a woman can do equally well. It was up to those who held the power and made the rules to accommodate women on an equal footing in the context of peacetime social reconstruction. This they signally failed to do.

Domestic life resumed, 1949
photo: BBC Hulton

3. 'NOW MISS, YOU MUST NOT MAKE AUGUSTA A BLUE': THE EDUCATION OF GIRLS.

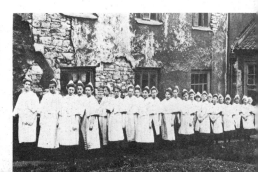

Orphanage, Bristol, c.1900
photo: BBC Hulton

Graduation Day
photo: Henry Grant

My dear lady, if my daughters were going to be bankers it would be very well to teach arithmetic as you do, but really there is no need.

So wrote a father to the headmistress of the newly founded Cheltenham Ladies College in 1860. It was a typical parental response of the time to the innovative notion that higher education should be available for girls. The idea that scientific subjects, applied or pure, are outside the 'needs' and by implication the capabilities of women, has still not been expunged. The Crowther report on education in 1959 observed: 'It is sometimes almost implied that no girl is interested in physics or mathematics and no boy in biology or English literature.'

Now the dissuasion is implicit, for ostensibly girls do have equal educational opportunities. Eighty per cent of children go to state co-educational comprehensive schools. Education is compulsory from 5 to 16. The same syllabuses are open to both sexes. The Sex Discrimination Act of 1975 covers state and independent schools, universities, polytechnics and colleges of further education. It makes less favourable treatment of boys and girls in any subject an offence. Local authorities must not, for example, provide better science facilities in boys' schools or discriminate in the award of grants. On the face of it girls are equally free to attend metalwork or needlework classes, to study physics or domestic science. However, girls tend to focus their attention – or more to the point have their attention focused – on a narrow range of subjects. 'Girls' subjects' are literature, languages, history, biology, sociology and domestic subjects. 'Boys' subjects' are maths, physics, chemistry and economics.

Seventeen per cent of all girls follow no science course at all in the fourth and fifth year of school. Thirty per cent less girls than boys take ordinary-level mathematics, though this or its equivalent is an essential qualification for careers in computer programming, technology, dentistry, architecture, horticulture, engineering, market research, printing, radiography, chemistry, economics, surveying, town planning, banking, among many other fields. (On the other hand in 1985 the youngest ever Oxford University mathematics scholar was a girl.) Women make up 5 per cent of undergraduates studying engineering and technology, 30 per cent of undergraduates studying science subjects and 64 per cent of undergraduates studying languages, literature and the arts. For every hundred boys passing ordinary-level technical drawing there are two girls, and only 23 per cent of ordinary-level physics passes go to girls.

Ratios like these are to be found at all levels of education. The problem is that 'girls' subjects' are less useful when it comes to career prospects, particularly at a time of microchip revolution. It seems that boys are educated with the clear understanding that this correlates with employment, or the hope of it, while the domain for girls is still assumed to be marriage, the home, social and domestic life. And this despite the fact that women now do paid work for most of their adult lives. Neglect of scientific and technical subjects severely limits their chances of skilled and well-paid jobs. There is more likelihood of earning a living from engineering than history. There are more prospects for technical workers than typists.

Ideas of girls' direction and the quality of their concerns are suggested in classrooms from very early on. In the Ladybird reading series 'Things We Like':

> Peter has a red ball.
> He plays with the boys with the red ball.
> Jane looks on.
> That was good, Peter, says Jane.

In **A Room of One's Own** Virginia Woolf wrote that for centuries women had been serving as looking glasses for men, reflecting them at twice their normal size – that is, that they enhanced the image of men while diminishing themselves.

Mothercare class
photo: Angela Coombes

A working party on sex differentiation in schools, set up in 1980 by the Schools Council, the body responsible until 1983 for advising on curriculum development, found that girls have much lower career expectations than boys of comparable ability:

> The issue is not that every girl must turn her back on traditional occupations and become a carpenter or an airline pilot. It is that all pupils should be exposed from a very early age to the possibilities which are available.

Dissuasion is communicated in all manner of ways. The Oxford Children's Reference Library book **Science**, for example, shows 107 men and boys in its illustrations and 17 women and girls. The men are involved in a variety of active and scientific pursuits, while the women do things like vacuuming, or mixing a pudding. No doubt the presentation is unconscious, and rooted in the bias of what constitutes femininity and the supposed range of interest of the 'female mind'.

'Female Knowledge'

That nineteenth-century father knew without asking them that his daughters were not going to be bankers. No doubt he also knew without asking them what their educational 'needs' were. These were assumed to be moral, religious, social and domestic. A preparation above all for wifehood and motherhood. In the 1860s long hours of needlework were compulsory for girls in elementary schools. In 1875 grants were provided for them to study domestic subjects – cooking, laundering and so on – after pressure from organizations like the National Association for the Promotion of Housewifery.

The highest expectation possible for most nineteenth-century women was to marry prosperously. The only profession open to 'well-bred' impoverished spinsters was that of governess. This was a rather dismal alternative to the marriage meal ticket. The women had no proper training or education and the profession was hugely overcrowded. A typical post in 1862 had 810 applicants for a subsistence salary of £15 a year. Queen's College for Women, the first college of higher education for women, was founded in 1848 to improve the training and prospects of governesses. Its objective was to teach 'all branches of female knowledge'. 'We are aware,' said one of its founders, 'that our pupils are not likely to advance far in Mathematics, but we believe that if they learn really what they do learn, they will not have got what is dangerous, but what is safe.' Presumably 'male knowledge' would have been 'dangerous', giving women ambitions outside their scope. For the few who gained access to it, it did. In 1841 Byron's daughter, Ada Lovelace

> transcribed a paper describing the analytical engine (the forerunner of the computer) written by General L. F. Menebrea . . . and in doing so added extensive translator's notes which amounted to an explanation of the manner in which the machine would be programmed . . . Her ideas were built on a century later to become some of the underlying principles in computer programming.

Trevor Williams (ed.),
A History of Technology,
Clarendon Press, 1978

Domestic science class, 1908 photo: GLC

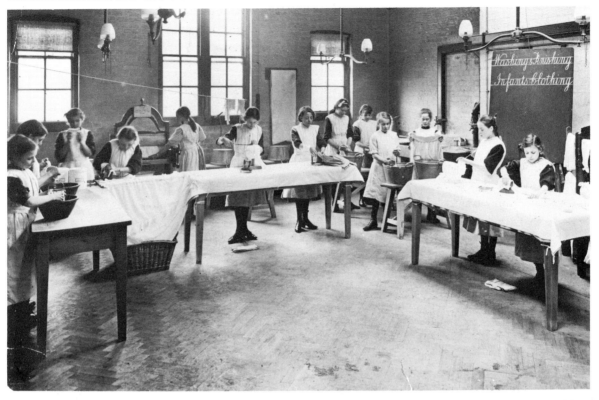

Cookery class, c.1910 photo: GLC

Despite the pressures on women in those days to keep in their place, a heroic few achieved academically against the odds, or pioneered educational reform and progress for women.

In the 1870s Elizabeth Garrett Anderson, sister of the suffragist Millicent Fawcett, defied the medical establishment to become the first recognized woman doctor in Britain. She had to take her examinations in Paris. The *Lancet*, the publication of the medical profession, was still maintaining that 'women's sphere in medicine should certainly be limited to carrying out the desires and implicitly obeying the dictates of male doctors'.

Dorothea Beale, the first headmistress of Cheltenham Ladies' College, aimed 'to provide an education which was worthy of comparison with the boys' public schools, but which was specifically for girls'. She taught science and geography and was considered radical and dangerous, though she made no overly powerful claims for girls. 'I desire to institute no comparison between the mental abilities of boys and girls,' she wrote in 1865, 'but simply to say what seems to me the right means of training girls so that they may best perform that subordinate part in the world to which I believe they have been called.'

In 1850 Frances Mary Buss, then aged 28, founded the North London Collegiate School for Girls, which was so well thought of that all high schools for girls opened after that date were modelled on it. She wanted to give her pupils sound teaching, physical exercise and outside examinations. This she did, in a world which derided such provisions and thought them dangerous, masculine and unnecessary. She saw dependence and ignorance as evils:

The terrible suffering of the women of my own class for want of a good elementary training have more than ever intensified my earnest desire to lighten, ever so little, the misery of women brought up 'to be married and taken care of' and left alone in the world destitute. It is impossible for words to express my fixed determination of alleviating this evil – even to the small extent of one neighbourhood alone.

Ray Strachey,
The Cause,
G. Bell, 1928

Emily Davies founded Girton, the first women's college at Cambridge, in 1873. She wrote of how her students ran the gauntlet of social disapproval to study there:

I am more and more impressed with the difficulties of conscience in the ways of young women as I hear about them. They think they ought not to urge their own wishes against those of their parents who, as Miss E. says, 'don't see the use of learning such a lot'.

Barbara Stephen,
**Emily Davies and
Girton College**,
Constable, 1927

In the 1860s Anne Jemima Clough arranged travelling lecture tours for poorly equipped and staffed schools, created the North of England Council for Promoting the Higher Education of Women, and in 1880 founded Newnham College, Cambridge.

'Cruel Injustice'

A Schools Enquiry Commission, set up in 1864 to report on middle-class education, found:

There is a long-established and inveterate prejudice that girls are less capable of mental cultivation and less in need of it than boys; that accomplishments and what is showy and superficially attractive are what is really essential for them; and that as regards their relations to the other sex and the probabilities of marriage, more solid attainments are actually disadvantageous. It must be fully admitted that such ideas have a very strong root in human nature . . . The appropriation of almost all the educational endowments of the country to the education of boys is felt by a large and increasing number both of men and women to be a cruel injustice.

The commissioners who made this enquiry also found 'mighty evidence to the effect that the essential capacity for learning is the same in the two sexes'. They recommended that girls' secondary schools, with Latin and maths on the curriculum, be set up in every town with 4,000 inhabitants or more, and that women be given the same opportunities as men when it came to higher education. A series of girls' public day schools followed, modelled on the boys' schools. They were for middle-class girls and were fee-paying, but fees were moderate and the curriculum wide. There were 38 of them by 1901. High schools for girls, such as Manchester High School, were founded too, and public schools for boarders were set up.

Such relatively recent reforms for women were achieved in opposition to the accepted social view of the capabilities of the female mind. Attitudes

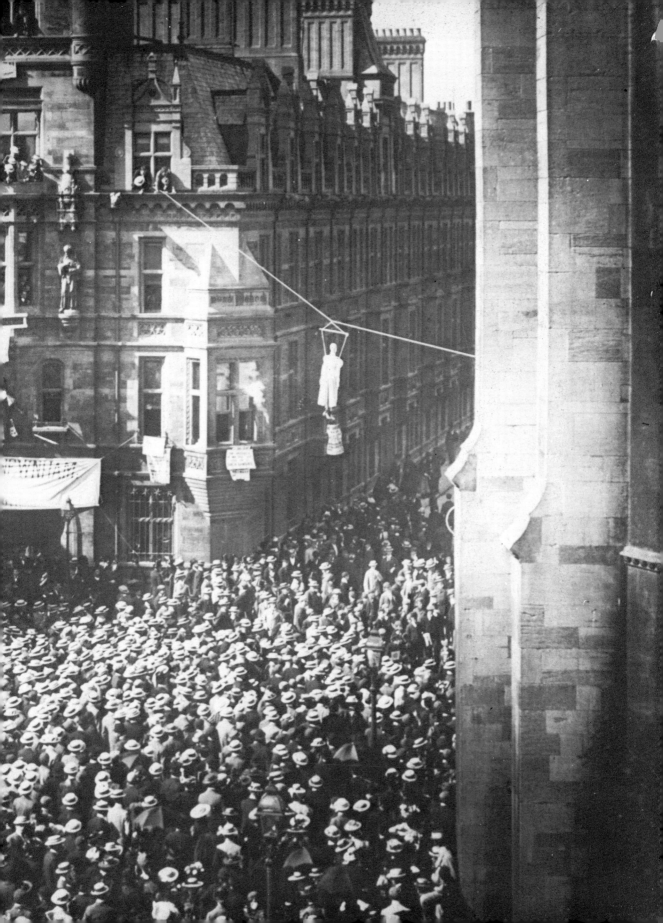

were as great a barrier to progress as opportunity. It was convenient to persist with the man-made myth that women had an innate incapacity for mathematics and science, for logic, economics, management, philosophy and the affairs of the world. The ignorant present no challenge. Often parents would actively discourage academic interest in their daughters for fear of jeopardizing their marriage chances. 'Now, Miss, you must not make Augusta a blue,' as one mother put it. No husband in his right mind, it was feared, would tolerate being upstaged by an intellectual wife, and the fate of an unmarried woman was thought dessicated and odd. Among the well-to-do, the eligible woman was one who would be a credit to her husband. She would have enough education to be socially gracious, she might sing, dance and paint a little, but her abilities and talents should be a domestic affair. Those opposed to reform looked to the traditional school curriculum to reinforce their concepts of lady-like behaviour, role definition and female identity.

Real ladies must have servants, as all the world knows. Class privilege – or lack of it – has bedevilled children's prospects down the years, and for working-class girls it was and is a double bind. Even today, children from professional or managerial backgrounds are ten times more likely to be in full-time education at the age of 18 than children whose parents do manual and unskilled work. Sixty per cent of adult women and 49 per cent of adult men have no educational qualifications. To them, for the most part, go the dull and low-paid jobs. At the beginning of the century education for middle-class girls lacked policy or cohesion, but it was possible to find a school if father paid the fees. Working-class girls – and that was most girls – went to elementary schools, where they were offered the rudiments of literacy and numeracy and a great deal of needlework, cookery, laundering and housewifery. They were servants in the making. The 1911 Census showed that 35 per cent of girls in full-time employment were doing jobs like hotel, laundry work and charring. In 1926 a Board of Education report, **The Education of the Adolescent**, advocated expansion of the housecraft syllabus for girls. 'Greater efficiency in the housewife would go far to raise her status in the estimation of the community,' it observed, without seeing the need to define the community that held housewifery in low esteem.

Concepts of what women are or should be like are hard to change. They are passed on by daughters who become mothers, pupils who become teachers, for generation after generation.

> When girls are invited to undertake domestic chores 'just like Mummy', the utensils on offer – half-sized irons, cookers, vacuum cleaners – supply no scope for the management, marshalling and manipulation which are implicit in the public character of the boys' equivalents: toy soldiers, model railways, garages and race tracks. While boys explore an expanding range of possibilities, girls serve a brief, narrow, private apprenticeship.

Marion Glastonbury,
The Times Educational Supplement, 1980

Even in the Second World War, when women worked as oxy-acetylene welders and motor mechanics, there was an assumption that they were acting the part – that they were sheep in wolves' clothing. **Munitions Girl: The Handbook of the Industrial Army** had a chapter patronizingly called 'Doing Sums':

If you do not like the look of this chapter, skip it, but sometime, if you have nothing to do, take a scrap of paper, a pencil and ruler and start reading it. Use the pencil to write down the figures and you will find they have no terror for you.

The time-honoured assumption is that anything to do with numeracy has profound and inbuilt terror for women, only to be overcome by coaxing and soothing. The historic myth of women's intellectual limitations, the tease that has a serious edge, the self-deprecating refusal to risk failure, the over-emphasis of the domestic context – all are effective deterrents to achievement. There is a probability that the new technology too will become a masculine preserve, with women, like high-tech housewives, doing the lowly jobs – screenwatching and dusting the hardware.

Academic recognition at university level was achieved for women in a piecemeal way. It was not until the 1944 Education Act that elementary, secondary, technical and university education were perceived as one continuous progression to which all who were judged able should have access. Women could take degrees at the University of London in 1878 (though not in medicine, they had to wait a few more years for that), and at Oxford in 1920. At Cambridge they could attend certain lectures from 1872 on, but it was as late as 1948 before they were allowed to take degrees on equal terms with men. Cambridge men voted in 1897 on women's right to graduate from the University. They voted no.

Students at the Slade, 1904
photo: Slade School of Art

If given the BA they must next have the MA and that would carry with it voting and perhaps a place on the Electoral Roll, a vote for the University Livings and all the rest. Even the BA Degree would enable them to take five books at a time out of the University Library on a ticket countersigned by 'their tutor'. I am entirely opposed to the admission of women to privileges of this character. And I honestly believe they are better off as they are.

W. B. Skeat,
quoted in
Rita McWilliams-Tullberg,
**Women at Cambridge:
A Men's University –
Though of a Mixed
Type**,
Gollancz, 1975

No sex discrimination was intended at the many new universities established after the 1938–45 war, but as late as 1963 only one 'redbrick' undergraduate in four was a woman.

The Hidden Dissuaders

For years the focus of struggle was for girls and women to be accorded places at schools and universities. The fact that women's achievements got scant mention in the man-made syllabuses went, if not unnoticed, then more or less unchallenged. Some feminists now question the whole framework of knowledge as it is taught:

Why is the substance of the curriculum almost exclusively white men and why, so often, does this go unnoticed or unchallenged? And why is it that the introduction of material on women and blacks is so frequently viewed as *political* when so much unmitigated nonsense on white men is given the stamp of approval, placed in halls of learning, is revered and called 'objective knowledge' and 'accumulated wisdom'?

Dale Spender,
**Invisible Women:
The Schooling
Scandal**,
Writers and Readers, 1982

Women's achievements, past and present, are now better chronicled. There are demands for the reshaping of history syllabuses to include women's history too. 'Women's studies' is an approved subject. Feminist sociologists advocate 'sex-role stereotyping intervention programmes' and the like, and teachers are dismantling the Wendy houses in nursery schools – or encouraging boys to use them too.

Research has shown that it is untrue that words like 'mankind' or 'he' are accepted by everyone as generic terms which necessarily include women. Under experimental conditions, schoolchildren illustrate stories about 'primitive man' with drawings of men to whom they give unambiguously male names. Even among university students, who are presumably more aware of linguistic conventions, the word 'man' is usually taken to mean just that. This was shown to be so in a study of college students asked to select appropriate illustrations for a sociology textbook. Those given chapter headings such as 'Social Man', 'Industrial Man' or 'Political Man' produced pictures of adult men engaged in social, industrial and political activity. Others given the titles 'Society', 'Industrial Life' and 'Political Behaviour' chose many more illustrations showing girls as well as boys, women as well as men. And in every form of teaching material there are more images of men than women.

Some intended progress paradoxically backfires. For example, the move to comprehensive education in the sixties seemed like an equalizing measure. Most children now go to co-educational schools. But girls in single-sex schools do better at maths and science subjects than those taught with boys. In mixed classes boys apparently receive a disproportionately high share of the teachers' time – even if only by being naughtier. Most teachers in secondary schools say they prefer to work with boys. Girls are described as more reticent and less demanding of attention.

Equal opportunities legislation, the acceptance in principle of a meritocratic view of education, concerted attempts to counteract prejudice and sex bias all have good effects, though progress is slow. Many parents now regard the employment prospects of girls and boys as of equal importance. And when it comes to examinations, girls are catching up fast. At the age of eleven they do better, on average, at all subjects than boys. So much so that some local authorities, including the Inner London Education Authority, use higher pass marks for girls in the comparability tests at the end of primary school. At ordinary level they get 51 per cent of all General Certificate of Education passes. At advanced level they get 46 per cent of all passes, and this percentage has increased yearly as more girls take the exams. In the universities, 41 per cent of undergraduates and 31 per cent of postgraduates are women.

Predictably, reflecting the nationwide tendency for women to be in the less influential, less prestigious, less well-paid jobs, far fewer women than men are involved at policy-making and managerial levels in the education system. Though 45 per cent of secondary school teachers are women, only 16 per cent of headships go to them. In primary schools the ratio is 77 per cent of teachers and 44 per cent of heads.

Outside the school system, in adult education, women are the keener pupils. Fifty-seven per cent of students attending part-time adult education classes are women. The Open University, founded in 1969, allows those without university entrance qualifications to study for a degree at home. Three times more women than men follow its courses; 30 per cent of new students classify themselves as 'housewives' when they enrol. It seems that women, caught as they are with the often isolating jobs of childcare and housework, learn for its own sake when they find the time.

After School

A number of state training schemes have been devised since the 1970s in response to unemployment – higher now than in the 1930s. In the last ten years unemployment for 16- to 19-year-olds has risen by 500 per cent for boys and by 700 per cent for girls. Schemes have titles like Youth Training Scheme, New Opportunities for Women, Wider Opportunities for Women. Policy statements for these schemes favour new horizons in women's employment. Girls and women join the YTS and the NOW and the WOW schemes, but the economic reality is that many cannot find work at the end.

And, whatever the intentions, the old polarizations occur. Girls are doing the courses in clerical work, secretarial skills, community care, education, food preparation, hairdressing. The boys are in the training workshops and skill centres, learning engineering, vehicle repair, carpentry and joinery, capstan setting,

Bank training class, Surrey
photo: Pete Addis

machining and bricklaying. Girls represent 1 per cent of students studying metalwork and engineering, 2 per cent in carpentry, 0·5 per cent in welding and construction, 1·5 per cent in heavy goods vehicle driving, 8 per cent in science and technology and 18 per cent of those on the management courses. On the other hand they make up 97 per cent of students on the shorthand typing courses, 74 per cent in hairdressing and catering and 63 per cent in office machine operating courses.

The unfortunately named Manpower Services Commission – the architect of the state training policy – published a report in 1979 on opportunities for women and girls in its training programmes. It stressed ways in which women could be introduced into 'non-traditional' areas of work. There are, it said, 'practically no jobs which cannot be done by girls given the opportunity and appropriate training'. It recognized women's particular disadvantages of lack of confidence and lack of technical and mathematical skills. It faced the problems of older women with domestic responsibilities. But as usual practice failed to match up to stated policy.

A key part of MSC schemes is to place trainees with employers so that they get work experience. Sponsors can only be encouraged, not forced, to make provision for women in 'non-traditional' areas of work. Employers, particularly in small firms, are notorious for their maintenance of segregated work roles. Nor are course selectors necessarily prejudice-free:

Art class
photo: Ian Berry

Alice and me applied for the TOPS course in carpentry and joinery. Two blokes took the interview. First bloke starts talking about the toilet. He was very unhappy about the fact that we would have to share the male toilet . . . The next thing was the fact that I wouldn't be able to get a job . . . Mr X then went on to say that I was taking a very real risk that I'd be raped while on the course. That there's no guarantee of the behaviour of sixty to a hundred blokes and there's bound to be one or two rotten eggs.

Quoted in Marion Lowe,
Education and Training,
Women's Rights
Information Sheets,
NCCL, 1981

The roots of inequality lie deep. Girls naïve enough to expect equality of opportunity at work, soon find out that the world of work favours men. Young women are not seen as any great investment – only 18 per cent of young people aged 16 to 19 released by their employers during working hours for part-time study are women.

Metalwork class
photo: Sally and Richard Greenhill

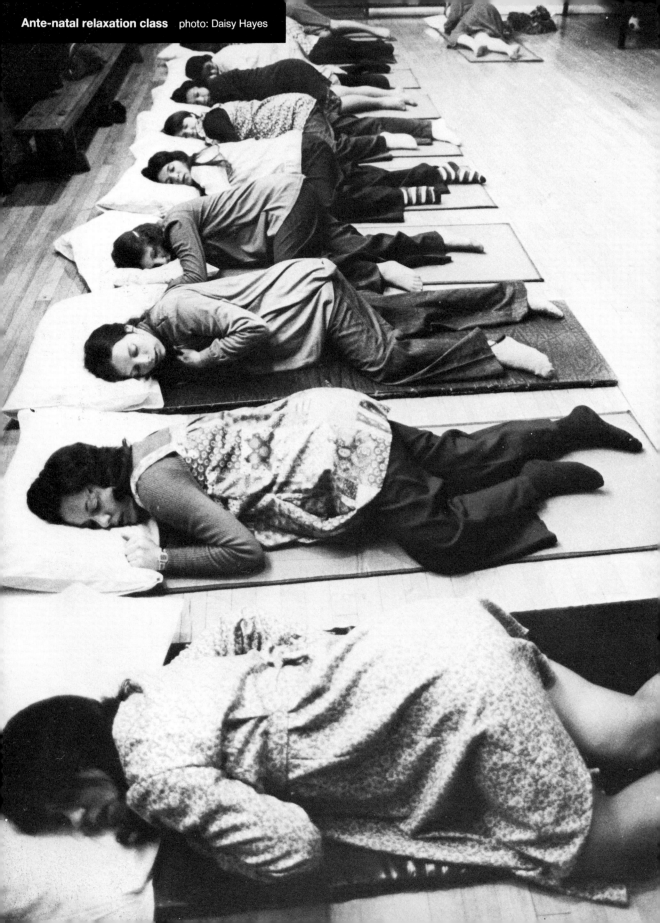

4. LIFE BEYOND THE NAPPY BUCKET: WOMEN AND THE FAMILY.

London street
photo: Jürgen Schadeberg

Wedding day
photo: Christine Voge

Advertisements for life assurance, perfect holidays and stain-free clothes project an image of the typical British family of father the breadwinner, mother the housewife and their two tousle-haired children – usually a boy and a girl. Sometimes there is a silver-haired grandma in the background. This happy little group shows up again and again in children's stories, television commercials, magazines, films and popular fiction until it has become *the* family snapshot in most people's minds. In reality it accounts for only 5 per cent of the population, though it stays entrenched as the prototype unit for which things like the family car and the family house are designed.

The other 95 per cent yields no cohesive picture of who is living with whom, under what contract and for how long. Relationships are more openly seen as shifting and complicated than ever before. There is no longer a stable family model to which most people conform. As the Study Commission on the Family sanguinely puts it: 'It is becoming less and less useful and valid to talk about the typical or average family. It is the diversity of family life that is typical.'

This diversity arises from all manner of influences and new-found freedoms. The Divorce Reform Act of 1969 means that ending a failed marriage need no longer be regarded as reneging on an agreement with God. Nor does it depend on proving the violence, licentiousness or insanity of one or other of the partners. After decades of campaigning, reasonably reliable contraception can be obtained free from the National Health Service and free, safe abortion is now available to many, though not all, who need it. Women have moved into the labour market and so increased their chances of economic independence from men. Technological advances like freezers, washing machines and central heating systems mean that more people can 'keep house' for themselves and that, as the American feminist Charlotte Perkins Gilman remarked, 'a house does not need a wife any more than it needs a husband'. More equal education opportunities have led to a revision upward of what life might yield for women. Post-war immigration has brought into the community people from other countries with different lifestyles and concepts of relationship. The gay and lesbian liberation movements have challenged assumptions about acceptable sexual relationships. Advances in medicine have led to a dramatic increase in life expectation – particularly for women. And of course the women's movement, with its massive publishing output, its reappraisal of women's worth, its slogans, banners, marches, committees, seminars, its protest at injustices, its calls for expression on all levels by women, about women and for women, has led to a challenge to the history of male domination and the notion that a woman must necessarily be a wife.

So it is that sex for most people is something other than a prerequisite for having babies, that increasing numbers of people 'cohabit', as government jargon puts it, that people live alone if they so choose, that married couples may divorce simply because they no longer get on with each other, and that single women of all classes can elect to have a child or children outside of marriage without that child being stigmatized as a poor little bastard and its mother as a fallen woman. 'Single-parent family' is the phrase that socially legitimizes a lifestyle that would have incurred ostracism not many years ago.

Marriage

Despite and within all this flux and freedom, 93 per cent of women in present-day Britain get married at some stage in their lives – more than in any other period of history. In mid-Victorian England, for example, a third of 'nubile' women stayed chaste and single, mainly due to a shortage of men. Those that married remained so, despite any reluctance as the years passed, 'till death them did part'. There was no legal or economic way out for women until 1857. The state's view remained that of the seventeenth-century Judge Hide:

If a married woman, who can have no goods of her own to live on will depart from her husband against his will, let her live on charity, or starve in the name of God.

Judge Hide in the case of Manby v. Scot in the reign of Charles II, quoted in R. Strachey, **The Cause**, G. Bell, 1928

In fact, married women had no independent legal status at all:

By marriage the very being or legal existence of a woman is suspended, or at least it is incorporated or consolidated into that of the husband, under whose wing, protection and cover she performs everything and she is therefore called in our law a feme covert.

W. Blackstone, **Commentary on the Laws of England**, 1765

Thus, a woman's property and earnings belonged to her husband. If he left her, she had no rights of custody over their children. She had no right to leave his house without his permission. Right up until 1925, if she committed a crime, other than high treason or murder, in his presence, his coercion was presumed and she was deemed innocent.

When legislation for divorce was finally introduced, it was still on an unequal basis. The Marriage and Divorce Act of 1857 stipulated that any man might divorce his wife for adultery, but that provision did not apply to women too:

It was 'natural' that a man should be unfaithful, and a woman must be expected to put up with it. If, however, the husband added cruelty, or desertion, or other crimes to his 'lapse', she might divorce him. And divorced people might legally remarry.

R. Strachey, **The Cause**

Wedding day, West Yorkshire   photo: Martin Parr

Today there are plenty of men available and marriage is easy, provided you are over 18 (or over 16 with parental consent), have the fee, a couple of witnesses and are not already spliced. But separation and divorce are easy too, and despite the popularity of marriage, new patterns of relationship have evolved and are continuing to do so. It is possible and increasingly probable that the same woman will, at different times in her life, live by herself, with a lover or lovers, with a husband or consecutive husbands, and with a child or children inside or outside of marriage. The handicaps of sexual secrecy and guilt are fast being shed. An increasing number of lesbians openly declare their sexual identity in an effort to make society accept their feelings as a fact of life. And extra-marital sex, though it still snaps the careers of politicians, is not the sin it was. Fear of sexually transmitted disease is now a greater deterrent to casual sexual liaison than fear of pregnancy or of not finding a husband when virginity is lost. The days when only virgins wed are long since past. Indeed it seems the days when virgins wed are decidedly on the wane. Nine out of ten young people feel that sex before marriage is acceptable and apparently over half the 65-year-olds agree. Views about what constitutes a 'good marriage' have modified. The contractual bargain of commitment has to feel all right and the thinking seems to be that it is better to base it on some experience. The average age for first marriage rises by the year. It currently stands at 24 for women and 26 for men. One in five couples who marry for the first time are already living together under the same roof.

Freedom and equality have become persistent themes for women, who are less likely to stay put in an unsatisfactory domestic set-up. One in three marriages now ends in divorce. Sixty per cent of couples divorcing have children under 16. England and Wales have the highest divorce rate in Europe. Alternative lifestyles are available. Women feel freer to live alone, to put their energies into paid work or study, or to find somebody new and perhaps more suitable. Divorced or separated they fare far less well economically, but it seems that the value put on emotional well-being is increasing all the time. Expectations from relationships are greater than they ever were and if these are unfulfilled – well then, the grass might be greener. An increase in divorce is not necessarily to be equated with an increase in unhappy marriages.

Of course, put another way – and it seldom is – two out of three married couples stay together until the death of one of the partners. This, despite longevity, temptation, new-found freedoms, easy divorce laws and the observable behaviour of others. This says a great deal for the strength of the institution of marriage – whether this comes from the value still put on long-term commitment or from the pressures that make escape seem impossible.

An essentially female identity has always been given to the notion of the family – home is Mother's domain, the woman's place, the bosom of the family, not its chest. But, as Mother's self-image changes and her confidence grows – as she burns her apron, corporately voices her anger at getting lumbered with all the domestic chores, and shows determination to work at what suits her, get hold of a fair share of the nation's wealth and decide how many babies she will have, if any –

the moral right, certain politicians and certain churchmen shudder in alarm and invoke the good old days of Victorian values. They allude to the rising crime rate, juvenile delinquency, God's commandments and a woman's role; male politicians demur on whether it is proper to permit doctors to prescribe contraceptives to girls under 16 without parental consent.

Such issues are felt to touch on the ethical significance of human life and the moral basis of society. Mother's role is propounded as all-important and fundamental. She is the foundation of love, the bedrock of emotional stability and the provider of good food. Well perhaps she is, but she is also fast developing a multiple personality. She most likely goes out to work; she may well drink her beer in pints, dye her hair, like disco dancing and leave the washing up in the sink for somebody else. She is increasingly liable to have sex when *she* wants and with whom, to divorce, remarry or even choose to raise her children alone without getting married. She also lives longer than ever before – on average five years more than Father – thereby raising the question of who will look after her when she is elderly and frail.

If the rates of divorce and remarriage suggest disillusion with the first choice of partner, they do not, by any means, suggest disillusion with marriage as such. The divorce rate has risen by 600 per cent since the early sixties, but the rate of remarriage is equally high. One in three marriages is a remarriage for one or other of the partners and one in six is a remarriage for both. One child in five has divorced parents and one child in 20 lives with the natural mother and a stepfather. Eighty per cent of women under 30 who divorce marry again within five years. There is also a trend towards re-divorce, but it is not yet clear whether second marriages last longer than first, or what percentage of people, with the hope that springs eternal, go into the fray for a third time. Seventeen per cent of divorces in England and Wales involve partners where one or both have been divorced before.

Love

The 93 per cent of women who marry may have all manner of motives for giving legal sanction to a relationship: problems over work permits, struggles with the Inland Revenue, the child that is on the way, concealment of unorthodox relationships, impulsive whims and fears. But it is love that is the essential precondition for most marriages. Indeed love appears to be more popular than ever, though in heftily revised and mind-broadening forms. It has, it seems, come down from its ecclesiastical and universal heights and got itself focused on satisfaction and fulfilment within inter-personal relationships. Other motives for marrying meet with disapproval or scepticism from majority public opinion.

Love is meant to be anarchic, powerful and 'bigger than both of us' – or all of us. Love should be free to smite whom it will. There is a gradation of value attached to terms such as 'liking', 'fond of', 'fancying', 'attracted to', 'infatuated with', 'loving' and 'in love with', and it is the latter which is thought to be the real McCoy, the true thing, which insulates the relationship from competition, represents an end to waiting and leads to settling down. In reality, however, Mr and Ms Right regularly come from similar cultural, class, educational and economic backgrounds. No doubt there is a degree of pragmatism and caution unobtrusively directing this apparently torrid emotion. Once love has been transmuted by marriage, it is meant to bring the security of an ordered everyday life and result in companionship, continuity and babies. Most people still expect fidelity to be the cornerstone of their marriage, and the ideal of intimacy based on trust and shared experience lives on.

Love is sold hard to teenage girls and women through pop music – 'You're the one that I want . . .', 'All you need is love . . .' – magazines and advertising. It would be hard to imagine a whole literature for boys devoted to how to catch and please a girl, but in popular fiction girls are encouraged to look on love as their salvation and self-fulfilment, the answer, The End. The typical dénouement in a Barbara Cartland novel is for the heroine, limp with love, to get carried off like prey or a prize by the hero:

> 'I love you,' he murmured. 'God, how I love you!'
> 'Are you . . . sure?' Karina asked.
> 'More sure than I have ever been of anything in my whole life! Tell me again that you love me! I am so afraid of losing you!'
> 'I love . . . you,' she whispered, and now her voice, like his, was deep with the passion he had aroused in her – a passion she did not fully understand – she only knew that she thrilled with an almost unbelievable excitement at the demand of his lips and the touch of his hands.
> 'I want you!'
> Rising to his feet the Earl drew Karina from the sofa into his arms. 'You are mine!' he cried possessively. 'Mine now and for all time. You will never escape me again my darling! I will never let you go!' His lips were on hers, holding her captive.
> Then, as her arms went round his neck, drawing him close and still closer . . . he lifted her high against his heart and carried her through the open door into the shadows of the great white bridal bed!

 She should have asked for his views on shared housework and equal opportunities. Such guff presents to women an unworkable image of themselves – beautiful in appearance and safe in a stranger's arms. It also makes its authors into multi-millionaires. Similar definitions of salvation are proffered again and again in all the endless froth of Mills-&-Boon-type publishing, the teenage weeklies **Oh Boy**, **Jackie**, **Loving**, **My Guy**, and the massive short-story output from the racks of women's magazines – **Woman**, **Woman's Own**, **Woman's Realm**, **Woman's Weekly**, **Woman's World**.

Carefree Sex

The progression is from attraction to love then sex (or sex then love), cohabitation then marriage. For a third of brides and grooms this is a cycle that recurs. The next stage on, after marriage, is having babies, though 13 per cent of women achieve this out of wedlock. As with all aspects of family life, the business of birth is changing fast, with new-found freedoms, choices and trends.

Procreation is much revered, but the desire to impede pregnancy is even stronger. For thousands of years women have, whatever the ideological consensus of their time, resorted to jellies, pastes, gums, leaves, fruits, seed pods, sponges, beeswax, dung and worse in order to prevent conception. With an understanding of human reproductive physiology, ancient ideas and practices have given way to relatively safe and effective birth control techniques.

In 1922 a health worker in north London, Nurse E. S. Daniels, was sacked from her job for referring women to birth control clinics. Her dismissal was the catalyst for a campaign by women:

Birth control is woman's crucial effort at self-determination and at control of her own person and her own environment . . . No economic changes would give equality or self-determination to any woman unable to choose or refuse motherhood of her own free will.

Stella Browne,
letter to
the **Communist**,
19 August 1922

The pioneers of modern birth control, Stella Browne, Marie Stopes, Dora Russell, risked prosecution for their work. In 1922 the police seized all copies of a pamphlet called **Family Limitation** and brought obscenity charges against those concerned with its publication and distribution:

The pamphlet said, among other things, that women should have pleasure in sexual intercourse, a point which I observed was displeasing to the Bench, who were, perhaps, thinking of their wives and daughters. There was also a diagram showing how, with the finger, to place a Dutch pessary in the vagina. Obscenity, we were advised, lay in the fact that this might not be the woman's own finger. Not having a sufficiently dirty mind, this had not occurred to me or to others.

Dora Russell,
'The Long Campaign',
New Humanist,
December 1974

The obscenity charge was upheld, but in defiance of the courts the pamphlet was reprinted in 1924 without the offending finger and was not seized again. Meanwhile the Catholic press described birth controllers as 'the kind of women who visit matinées and sit with cigarettes between their painted lips'.

Peter Fryer,
The Birth Controllers,
Corgi, 1967

Stella Browne saw birth control as related to the problems of housing, lack of education and unemployment. It was also the key to new sexual ethics in which voluntary and conscious motherhood was fundamental, promoting 'honest and dignified relationships between men and women'. She made lecture tours throughout the country, at which 'every foot of floor space was packed and women, mostly with babies clasped in their arms, stood five deep in rows behind the chairs'.*

*F. W. Stella Browne,
'Birth Control in Taff Vale',
New Generation,
October 1923

How often in this tour have elderly women not said, 'You've come too late to help me, Comrade, but give me some papers for my girls. I don't want them to have the life I've had.'

F. W. Stella Browne,
'My Tour in
Monmouthshire',
New Generation,
January 1924

A report on the state of public health in 1933 estimated that one in seven pregnancies ended in illegal abortion. The birth control campaigners saw safe, prompt, legal abortion as a necessity to abolish 'the trail of disease and crippling injuries, displacements, discharges, haemorrhages, inflammations' brought about by illegal terminations.*

*See F. W. Stella Browne,
The Right to Abortion,
Allen & Unwin, 1935

An Abortion Law Reform Association publication of 1936 put the case with passion:

> What is this ban on abortion? It is a survival of the veiled face, of the barred window and the locked door, burning, branding, mutilation, stoning, of all the grip of ownership and superstition come down on woman, thousands of years ago.

Today services are widely available to ensure that every child should be a wanted child and sex itself a carefree affair. In 1974 contraceptives were made available, free of charge on the National Health Service, to everyone over 16 irrespective of marital status. Doctors may use their judgement on prescribing contraceptives to girls under 16 – 20 per cent of whom are sexually active – without parental consent.

Most married women use the pill, because it is a hundred-per-cent reliable, though there is now some anxiety over harmful side-effects with long-term use. The diaphragm, or Dutch cap – designed by a nineteenth-century Dutch physician, Aletta Jacobs – gives women day-to-day control over conception. Spermicides and condoms, of all hues and textures, can be bought over the counter or bulk-ordered by post. Sterilization for women and men is free and a recent Family Planning Association survey showed that more than 13 per cent of married women over 35 with children choose to be sterilized. The 1967 Abortion Act provided abortion free on the National Health up to 28 weeks of pregnancy if two doctors sign a form agreeing that the physical or mental health of the mother and family is at risk, or if the foetus is deformed. In 1985 the time limit was reduced to 24 weeks. In fact 80 per cent of all abortions take place before the twelfth week of pregnancy, and since the advent of safe, sterile, legal abortion, connected deaths of women are extremely rare. A quarter of all abortions are sought by teenagers and 35 per cent by married women – whose husbands do not have to consent. However, a great many women would like the abortion facility to be available to all women who, for whatever undeclared reasons, do not want to have the child.

Along with a reduction in the numbers of unwanted babies has gone a proliferation of agencies, clinics, counselling services, magazine 'agony aunts' and sex therapists all trying to ensure that, for the sheer hell of it, sex works. A woman's or man's sex life is now viewed separately from the business of having babies and the general climate of advice is that people should have the right to express themselves freely and the back-up services to help them so to do. No issue has more fundamentally affected women's lives than fertility control and such enlightened legislation as there is has been won by women who have campaigned for reforms.

Mothers and Fathers

Now that they can, for the most part, choose, women in England and Wales have remarkably few babies. The average married couple has 1·9, a record low. None the less almost 90 per cent of first-time marrieds do, by choice, have a child or children. The 10 per cent who are infertile regret the lack in their lives and seek to

Ante-natal relaxation class – for fathers too   photo: Daisy Hayes

Birth of twins   photo: Daisy Hayes

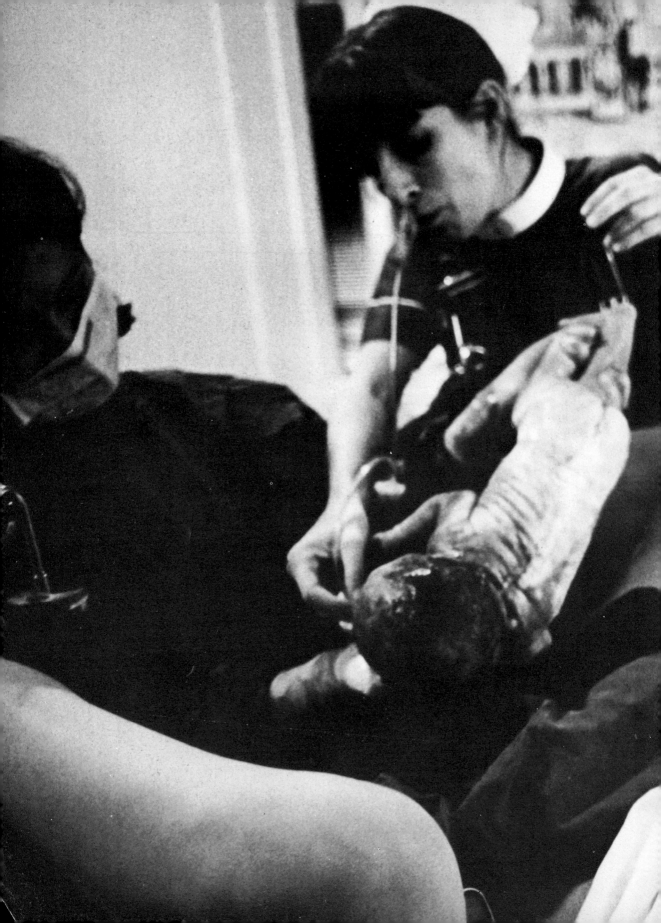

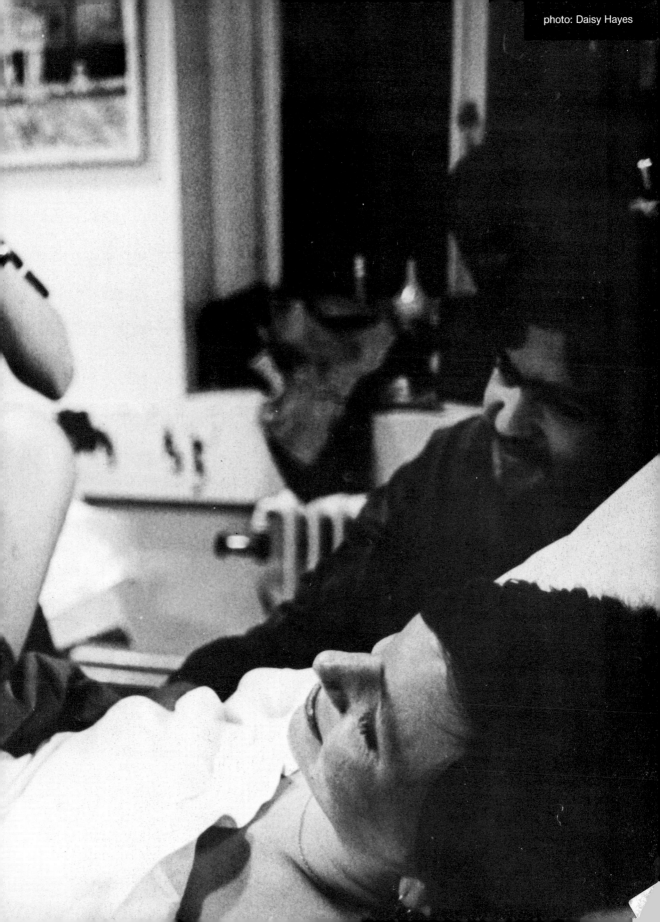

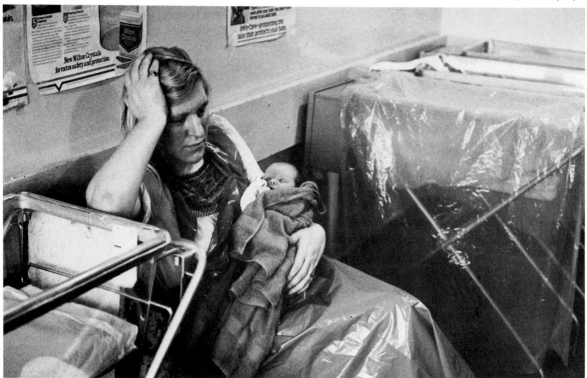

Leaving hospital

overcome it by fertility drugs, artificial insemination by donor, fostering or adoption.

Thirteen per cent of children are born to single women – a proportion that grows yearly. An increasing number of economically independent women elect to bring up a child alone. There is a growing group of lesbians who choose motherhood but also maintain relationships with other women. Half the births to teenage brides are conceived before marriage. It seems that diversity is the order of the day.

The average mother has her first child when she is 26 – two years after her marriage. She goes to ante-natal classes and nearly always has the baby in hospital with little risk to her life. Many women are critical of the 'production-line' atmosphere of modern maternity wards and press for a more natural approach to childbirth, but the grim historical scenes of maternal mortality are mercifully past. And father is increasingly present at the birth and encouraged to play a supportive role and share the experience of the arrival of the child.

His presence is evidence of some movement towards more equal relationships between women and men. In general, though, roles appear not to have changed as much as attitudes suggest. According to surveys, when it comes to that host of activities and skills known as 'housework', men are progressive in attitudes rather than actions. When his wife goes out to work a man raises his participation in housework by around half an hour a day. Playing with the children is the domestic activity most favoured by helpful husbands. On the other hand there are now twice as many single-parent families as there were in the early sixties, and one in nine single parents is a father on his own with his children.

Father feeding the baby
photo: Sally Greenhill

Post-natal class
photo: Daisy Hayes

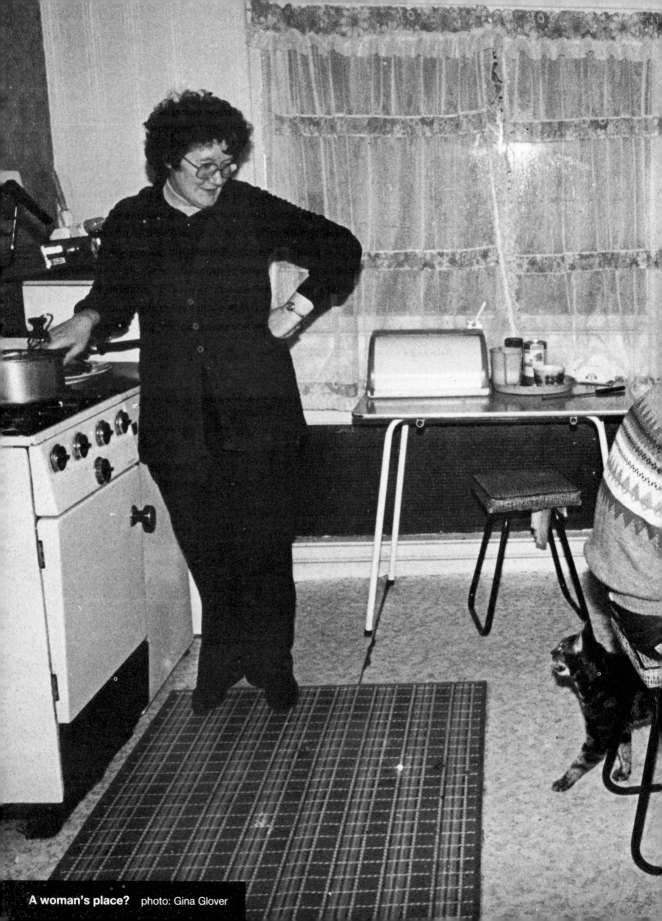

A woman's place? photo: Gina Glover

Day out, Lancashire photo: Paul Trevor

Single-parent family photo: Ed Barber

As most mothers go out to work – they comprise a quarter of the workforce – they now have double roles. They labour for money as secretaries, teachers, factory workers and nurses and they labour for love at home. If evaluated in economic terms, housework would represent 39 per cent of the Gross National Product. But because it overlaps with family life it is not taken seriously as work. 'I am only a housewife' is the self-denigrating remark of numerous women who have acquired all the numerous management and craft skills that homemaking demands. Safe working conditions in offices and factories are controlled by legislation, but the working conditions of housewives are no one's business but their own. Yet a third of all fatal accidents are domestic and the kitchen is the most dangerous room in the house. And though the development of household technology, improved living standards and the growth of a consumer society have taken the sheer arduousness out of household chores for most women, one in 20 British homes still has no bath or inside lavatory, one in three has no washing machine and half have no central heating.

Nor has technology significantly shortened the amount of time women spend on housework. The average housewife with young children puts in a 77-hour week. Predictably, those lower down the social scale have the hardest time. Money might not buy love, but it certainly helps when running a home. In one large study of mental health in London, 42 per cent of working-class women with children under six were classed as suffering from depression and were socially isolated and poorly housed. And there are only four full-day state care places for every hundred children under five. For the most part the children of working mothers are looked after by relatives, neighbours or paid childminders – with a dubiously unequal standard of care.

her and daughters, Cambridge

photo: Peter Espé

Though children now contend with few sibling rivals, their chances of having to come to terms with new-fangled familial relationships increase by the day. One in five children born today will, before their twelfth birthday, see their parents part. Chances are, each parent will then again 'cohabit' and remarry. The child will find its way through a dense family tree of euphemistic aunts and uncles, step-fathers, -mothers, -brothers, -sisters and -grandparents and half and quarter cousins.

Another group much affected by family flux is the old. Life expectation for women and men has increased dramatically. In 1900 one person in 80 was over 75 years old. Now the figure is one in 16, and this is expected to double in the next 50 years. Women are twice as likely as men to live this long; on average they outlive men by five years or so. This raises the question of whose job it is to care for the elderly, many of whom now live alone. Traditionally daughters looked after their ageing, ailing parents and all too often this is still the case, for state provision is poor. But the daughters themselves are now often far from young, or are out at work, or living far away, or asking themselves why they should do all the unpaid caring jobs. Nor is it yet clear whether relatives are equally concerned about ageing step-parents or ex-in-laws needing support.

Like much else in British life 'the family' is changing fast, with

89

all kinds of implications for social policy concerning work opportunities, housing, taxation, pensions, welfare benefits and so on. Governments embarrassed by record unemployment try to discourage women – by low wages and inadequate nursery facilities – in their move away from housebound housework and into the arena of paid labour. Much is heard at the present time of the importance of family life, but it is not clear quite what definition of 'family' is being used. If family life means living with a parent, child or spouse, then an awful lot of women live outside a family context and in quite different social relationships for all or large parts of their lives. It sometimes seems to be overlooked that the moral and social worth of a law-abiding lifestyle is no less because it is unfamiliar or innovatory. Leaders who consider marriage sacrosanct and sex a sin unless it is for making babies are unlikely to concede contraception, abortion and divorce for all who want it. But there is an ever-growing number of women who need to believe in life beyond the nappy bucket, who seek an expanding range of possibilities in education, work and all forms of expression, who have their sights set on equality of opportunity and achievement. For them, changes that offer more freedom, more choices, more open doors, are hard to win and, once gained, are tenaciously defended.

91

Margaret Thatcher
photo: Eve Arnold/Hillelson

5.

'PAY PEANUTS AND YOU GET MONKEYS': WOMEN'S WORK.

Pay day!
photo: Nick Hedges

The marked progress of the mid-seventies towards equal pay has come to a halt . . .

In every occupation men earn more per hour than women . . .

Women workers are heavily concentrated in relatively few occupations . . .

Women are seriously under-represented in public life, both in elected office and among public appointments . . .

Women remain poorly represented in most professions . . .

The proportion of women trade union members is not reflected in their representation on executive councils, among full-time officials and among delegates to the Trades Union Congress. Even with unions with a predominantly female membership, women are under-represented in these positions.

Equal Opportunities
Commission
Ninth Annual Report,
1984

The EOC's Annual Report, a statistical digest, depicts the relative positions of women and men in British society. The ninth, eighth, seventh, sixth, fifth and fourth reports show little variation where women's employment is concerned. To women invariably go the low-skilled, low-status, low-paid jobs.

Money is a metaphor for worth and esteem, but it is also exceedingly useful for buying the necessities and luxuries of life. The significance of pay in Britain is felt more than it is analysed. Its distribution changes marginally according to which political party is in power, but pay increases are usually determined as a percentage of what you already have. It does not take a mathematical witch or wizard to work out that 10 per cent of £600,000 a year is rather different from 10 per cent of £6,000 and that such a system of pay increases widens the gap between the rich and the poor.

Governments seem to accept that the unemployed and disadvantaged should have just enough in the way of cash benefits to keep them alive, but that luxuries like a car, carpets, reasonable clothing, central heating and a washing machine are not for them. At the other end of the scale 'the sky's the limit', as Margaret Thatcher said, for the entrepreneurs, the decision-makers and the 'captains of industry'. One per cent of the population own 20 per cent of the nation's wealth and 10 per cent of the population own 54 per cent of the wealth. To them go the villas in the sun, the hand-built limousines, the private jets. The beneficiaries are virtually all men, but no doubt they buy furs and jewels for their wives and mistresses.

The 'politics of envy' is decried as unworthy, but there was national recoil in 1985 when a 'top people's pay award' for the excessively well paid advocated percentage annual increases in themselves twice as much as most people earn. The objection was not to the principle of paying one man an inordinate amount and one woman very little. It was that it appeared insensitive and ill-timed to give whacking increases to the very rich a few days after a government ruling that proposed to abolish the wages councils, which had sought to safeguard the minimum earnings of the worst paid. Defending the 'top people's award', a Conservative politician said, 'Pay peanuts and you get monkeys.' He should have said pay peanuts and you get women.

'It's slave labour. With such a lot of unemployment around they know that women will work for washers.'

Woman working in a sausage processing plant, Sunderland

Washers or peanuts, there is a strong link between what are known as women's jobs and low pay. The 'top people's pay award' benefited generals, judges and high ranking civil servants. It did not much affect women. There are no Boadiceas around right now; 75 of the 78 High Court judges are men, and the Civil Service is remarkable for its concentration of women in the lowest grades. In 1984 the gross weekly earnings of women in the Civil Service averaged 66 per cent of men's. No Permanent Secretaries are women, only 4 per cent of Deputy Secretaries, 5 per cent of Under Secretaries and 10 per cent of Principals. Unsurprisingly, however, women make up 77 per cent of clerical assistants.

If, as is suggested, pay is concomitant with value, then the average woman is worth about two thirds as much as the average man. In every occupation employing significant numbers of men and women, men earn more per hour. The disparity varies from job to job. Policewomen earn 93 per cent as much per hour as policemen; women nurses and midwives get 90 per cent as much as their male counterparts; women storekeepers, cleaners, supervisors and clerks, 80 per cent; women sales staff, shop assistants and shelf-fillers earn 70 per cent; and women sales supervisors and machine operators about 66 per cent. Women's average hourly earnings in full-time jobs, excluding overtime, are 73 per cent of men's earnings. Their average weekly money, including overtime, is 66 per cent of men's – £116 as against £177. In 1976, soon after legislation on equal pay came into force, the ratio was £72 to £46, giving women 64 per cent as much as men. A 'bottom people's pay award' would principally concern women. It is in the crucial area of parity of pay that the least progress towards equality is being made.

As for pensions, women are far less likely to enjoy a retirement pension over and above the benefit levels offered by the state, even though they live, on average, five years or more longer than men and are compulsorily retired five years earlier. There are three times more widows than there are widowers and a third of all elderly women live on their own. Yet only 28 per cent of working women are eligible to belong to occupational pension schemes.

The Victorian adage was that 'a woman's place is in the home'. The spectre of the disintegration of the family is still called up when women's working rights are raised. This conditioned response is useful for entrenching male privilege. The facts belie the attitudes. Women *are* working. They constitute 42 per cent of the paid labour force. One in four workers is a married woman. Sixty-one per cent of married women aged between 16 and 59 are doing paid work or are registered as unemployed and are looking for work. It is cunning but unfair to restrict women's work prospects because of assumptions about their private lives – motherhood, domesticity and the rest. Most women get married and have children. But so do most men. Most women do the housework, but so could most men.

Child minder
photo: Gina Glover

Time to Work

The average married woman has one or two children and her life expectancy has rocketed to more than 75 years. Even if she accepts traditional role divisions and regards caring for the children as her responsibility, she at most devotes seven full-time years of her life to them if there is a two-year age gap between them and both start school at five. That leaves a lot of living. About half a century in fact:

> Is it wise or sensible to push those fifty years into the background, to create a situation where schoolgirls see that vast expanse of time as an unimportant miasma, simply for the sake of those important, harassing, hectic years that look as though they will never end, but do, in fact, soon come to an end?

Eva Figes,
Patriarchal Attitudes,
Virago, 1970

An encapsulating patriarchal statement about 'a woman's place' was made by Sir John Newsom when chairman of the Central Advisory Council for Education. He was defending the retrograde attitude to the education of girls contained in his official report on education:

> The influence of women on events is exerted primarily in their role as wives and mothers, to say nothing of aunts and grandmothers. Even in employment outside the home, with the exception of schools and hospitals, this influence usually works by sustaining or inspiring the male. The most superficial knowledge of the way in which the affairs of Government, industry and commerce are conducted makes this quite plain. What infuriates a rather esoteric group of women is that they want to exert power both through men and also in their own right, and that this is almost impossible.

Observer,
11 October 1964

The desires of that 'rather esoteric group of women' grow more universal by the day and it does now seem as if even that bland creation of the opinion polls 'Ms Average' believes that women must work because they need the money, that having a job is the best way to be independent and that it is possible to combine family responsibilities with paid work. Six thousand women were questioned in this 1980 survey done by the Office of Population Censuses:

	Agree	Disagree	Neither agree nor disagree
	%	%	%
A woman's place is in the home	25	57	18
ried women have a right to work if they want to, whatever their family situation	71	17	12
Most married women only work for pin money – they don't need a job	20	66	14
Women can't combine a career and children	29	55	16
If her children are well looked after, it's good for a woman to work	71	12	17
Having a job is the best way for a woman to be an independent person	67	16	17

These progressive views are at odds with what is on offer. Most children of working mothers are looked after by registered childminders, relatives and friends (themselves nearly all women, of course), and the quality of such care varies greatly.

The survey also found that 90 per cent of women expect either to continue working when they have children or to go back to work later. Only 4 per cent said they would not go back to work. It seems that women who hold the most traditional views of domestic destiny are older, non-working and have no children.

Husbands are less generous in their notions of a 'woman's place', but they too are revising their attitudes. Eight hundred married couples were questioned on the importance of the equality legislation of 1975:

	Proportion rating as 'very important'	
	Wives	Husbands
	%	%
The opportunity for boys and girls to study the same subjects at school	81	75
Equal credit and mortgage facilities for men and women	80	75
Laws giving men and women equal pay for equal work	73	70
The right to 6 weeks' maternity pay if a woman has been in her job for two years	72	64
Laws making it illegal to treat men and women differently at work	67	65
The right for a woman to return to her job within 6 months of having a baby	50	44

There are many similar surveys, statistics and analyses which show that people actually *want* equality – or say they do – and dislike systems that entrench male privilege and discriminate against women in such startling ways. For women, the debate is over as to whether they should or should not work, whether they are of equal ability, whether they should be equally rewarded. The debate now is why systems that perpetuate discriminatory practice continue to roll on undisturbed. Over the past 30 years there has been a 90-per-cent increase in the number of women going out to work. Most women do paid work for 70 per cent of their working lives. They do so because they need the money and because they want to. Very few women positively do not want to have a job. They are out in the workplace and there they are going to stay.

Banquet photo: Jürgen Schadeberg

Laundry workers, London photo: Maggie Murray/Format

The first woman fire-fighter   photo: Brenda Prince/Format

New kinds of work:

Plumber   photo: Jill Posener

Bus driver   photo: Brenda Prince

Archaeological diver   photo: Jill Posener

Women's publishing firm, London   photo: Ed Barber

Bicycle repair co-operative, London   photo: Ed Barber

Cinema of Women, film distributors   photo: Times Newspapers

Top Jobs and Female Ghettos

Women may be out at work, but they are dramatically excluded from all the jobs that command high salaries, power and visible decision-making – management, the professions, public and political life. They are denied the truly interesting jobs as well as the swank and the booty. The reason for this nationwide exclusion is clear. Men hold such jobs, have held them and intend to go on doing so. The whole theatre of high office, the board-rooms, the spacious desks, the company cars, the business lunches, expense accounts, investment programmes and management structures are not for the ladies. Secretaries are often executives exploited as sort of second-string wives. They sit in ante-rooms and must be keen to oblige. Office 'girls', tea 'ladies' and canteen staff – that is the female domain – and of course the women who come in at dawn to spray the telephones with some fragrance, clean up and empty the bins.

Women are absent from the power bases of public life. The affairs and institutions of society: politics, the law, the police, the army, the church, the stock exchange, manufacture, industry, agriculture – all were structured by men and are run by men, largely in the interests of men. They want their colleagues to be of the same class, colour and sex as themselves. They want them to be from the same schools and universities. 'Is he one of us?' is their reference. Details of dress and behaviour become coded signals of reliability – the stitching round the suit lapels, the way a knife and fork are held, the cut of the hair, are badges of compatibility. Women in such leading roles are seen as anomalous and as a sexual threat.

Some women, with cool voices and in business suits, do slip through, but the number is dismally small. One Cabinet Minister (the Prime Minister), three High Court judges and less than 1 per cent of directors of public and large companies. 'What about Margaret Thatcher?' people ask, but she is no help at all. It is extraordinary that the first ever British woman Prime Minister should have done so little for other women – should have opposed equality legislation, urged them, ludicrously, back to the kitchen sink, endorsed the abolition of legislation that sought to protect them from exploitatively low wages. Her identification is with the unbending patriarchal systems – the judiciary, the army, the police, the management arm. Her so-called meritocracy is really a power elite for the men who accrue the most money.

Meanwhile, women make up just under 2 per cent of 'high earners'. (In 1968 the percentage was just over 2 per cent.) Three per cent of the members of the British Institute of Management are women, 5 per cent of the Institute of Marketing, 7 per cent of the Institute of Chartered Accountants, 12 per cent of the Law Society (solicitors), and 25 per cent of the British Medical Association, which represents family doctors – the higher up the medical profession, the fewer women there are.

Since 1960 more women have trained for the professions and joined at junior levels, but most stay below their potential. Teaching is a telling example. Like nursing, it is a profession that has always employed a lot of women,

Nurse
photo: Ian Berry

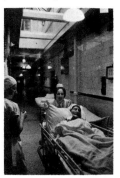

Doctor at London health centre
photo: Carlos Guarita

102

but they are concentrated in the lower-paid jobs. In nursery schools virtually all the teachers are women. In primary schools they account for 77 per cent of the teachers and 43 per cent of the heads and in secondary schools 44 per cent of teachers and only one per cent of heads.

Most women work in the service sector and in a few of the manufacturing industries. The ghettos of female labour in manufacturing are the clothing, textiles and footwear industries, food processing, electronics and to some extent printing and publishing. Women tend to do the boring, repetitive jobs: they are 60 per cent of all packers, bottlers, canners and fillers, 55 per cent of repetitive assembly workers, 82 per cent of electrical assembly workers. In the clothing industry all the machinists are women, while men do the more skilled jobs like cutting. Many jobs in the food processing industries are dull and unpleasant:

The work is smelly and boring. You just stand there all day doing the same thing over and over again – selecting the prawns, shelling the prawns. The money's OK. You can take home £70 in a good week when there's lots to do. The lasses are OK though.

Woman working in the food processing industry, Sunderland

It was in low-paid jobs with poor union representation that the wages councils did at least provide a safety net for pay rates.

The lowest earners in the land are black women. The discrepancy between the earnings of black and white women is not as great as between those of black and white men, because white women are themselves so poorly paid. Work rates for black women vary according to their background. A very high percentage of women of West Indian origin (74 per cent) work, as do a large number of non-Muslim Asian women – 45 per cent. However, only 17 per cent of all Muslim Asian women work, and only 9 per cent of Pakistani women. In general black women have less upward mobility and less promotion prospects than white.

still work in factories & as secretarys

New Technology

Dull and circumscribed though women's jobs might often be, they are for many a preferable alternative to the poverty and isolation of unemployment. The new technology hits hardest at the occupations in which most women work. A third of all employed women do clerical jobs. Electronic word and data processing mean that far fewer people are now needed to do the same amount of work. Virtually all typists and secretaries are women and it is estimated that 17 per cent of their jobs will be lost by 1990 because of word processing. In some cases staffing levels have already fallen by up to 50 per cent.

The introduction of cable networks over the next few years is also likely to accelerate office job losses. These networks will link up separate computer systems and in many cases eliminate paper-based systems altogether. The all-electronic office is not far away. Old clerical skills are fast becoming redundant. The new tasks assigned to women tend to be repetitive keyboard-tapping and screen-watching. Where new technology has created interesting and highly skilled new jobs, for instance in systems design, these have overwhelmingly been filled by men. For it

103

is men who receive the scientific and technical education and training which equips them to design and control the new technology.

In factories, where a quarter of all working women do semi-skilled and repetitive tasks, new technology is being introduced in the form of robots and computerized control and monitoring systems. Robots can do routine assembling, sorting and packing. In some industries, such as printing or clothing manufacture, new technology has been used not only to cut jobs, but also to break down the 'craft' component of jobs which had traditionally been men's and convert them into 'women's work'. Along with that conversion have, predictably, gone lower wages and lower status.

Women have had a lot of confidence knocked out of them by the stick of low pay. A good wage is a great boost to self-esteem. Men tend to be less patronizing if they know that women are on an equal salary rating. They are less likely to call them 'love' or 'ducky' and disregard their views. And women are more assertive if they are properly paid. Having been so long underrated, women tend to underrate themselves. If two similar jobs are advertised, one at £9,000 and one at £19,000 a year, they are more likely to apply for the former. One manager, who wanted an all-male workforce, sacked the women and then re-advertised their jobs at greatly increased salaries. No women applied.

The Double Shift

As well as doing paid work, 80 per cent of women are also still housewives in the sense that they have responsibility for running a home. They shop, cook, clean, care for men, children, the elderly and disabled in that unpaid, unvalued activity known as 'housework'. Much of their continuing financial dependence rests on their unpaid domestic labour. When governments dismantle the welfare state and talk of 'self help' and 'community care' women give a sideways glance. They know it means more work for them at home. And the assumption that domestic chores are 'women's work' shapes more than traditional family life. A great deal of the waged work women do outside the home is domestic in character – serving people, caring for them, looking after their physical and emotional needs. Such jobs are unrespected and poorly paid.

If women change or quit their jobs they usually do so for work-related rather than domestic reasons. None the less, the facts of mothering and home life are used to stymie their employment and promotion prospects. Employers assume that if women are young they'll get married and leave work, if they're married they'll have children and leave, and if they have children they'll leave because of them. And if none of these apply then there must be something odd about them. They use such projections as reasons for not employing women. It would be more useful to women were employers to revise their work structures: provide flexible working hours, adequate maternity leave, childcare facilities, job-sharing and part-time working schemes.

'If there was an important work meeting and your child was ill,

Community nursery, London   photo: Carlos Guarita

Early morning cleaners   photo: Jürgen Schadeberg

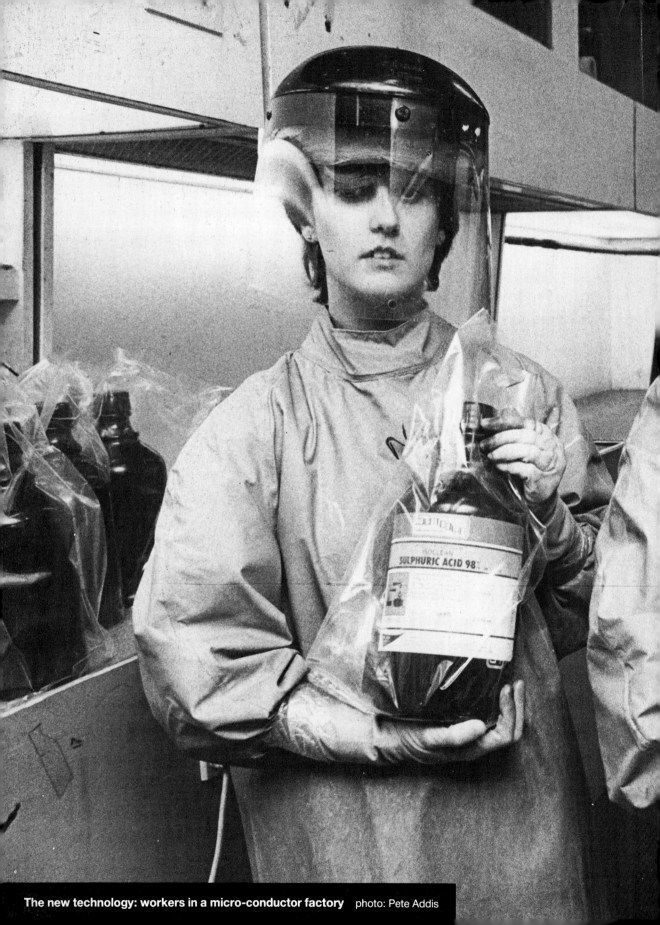

The new technology: workers in a micro-conductor factory   photo: Pete Addis

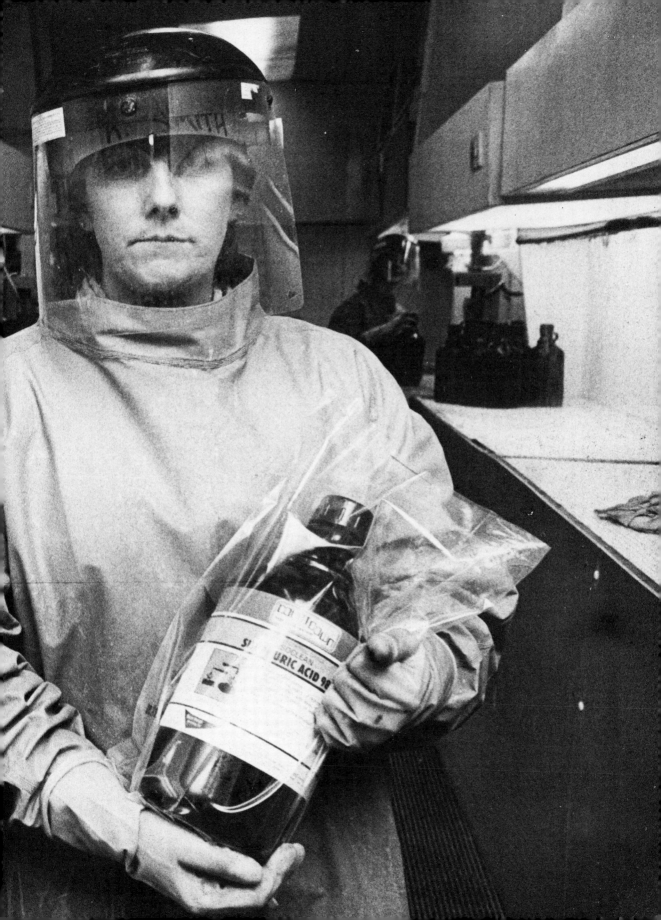

Boredom: factory worker, West Midlands   photo: Nick Hedges

which commitment would you choose?' is an often quoted trick question fired at women at interviews. It is asked so that the interviewer can rationalize his or her rejection of the woman candidate. Perhaps most men would choose their child too. Perhaps most men value their emotional and private lives more highly than their work. They are never asked. The projected scenarios are anyway invariably spurious. Most situations are more open-optioned than such questioning seeks to imply.

Until shared family responsibility is fully recognized and practised and until the provision of support services by the State is adequate, many women's working lives are dictated by the needs of their dependants.

TUC report, **Women in the Labour Market**, 1983

Forty per cent of working women have dependent children and many of these mothers work part time. Eighty-four per cent of all part-time work is done by women. They are employed in the same occupations as women full-time workers, but are paid rather worse and lose out on fringe benefits like holidays, sick pay, annual increments and pensions. And often the available work under-uses their skills and training. One in 25 women working part time in low-skilled catering and cleaning jobs has a teaching qualification, one in 12 has a nursing qualification and one in 6 has clerical and commercial training.

Homeworkers are the most disadvantaged of all. There are an estimated 400,000 homeworkers – nearly all women who cannot go out to work because they have small children or elderly relatives to care for. Women from some ethnic minorities face particular pressure to work in their homes. The jobs are sewing, typing, card-punching, packing. It is the worst paid of any kind of work. The workers are on piece rates or low hourly rates, often have to buy their own equipment, are socially isolated and not unionized.

Hardship is relative. Perhaps the woman working in a sausage factory for 'washers' regards that as better than being on the dole. Statistics of those out of work do not tell the full story because they are now based on a count of people claiming Unemployment Benefit. A lot of women – at least 270,000 in 1985 – are not entitled to any money, so do not claim. But even using this method of counting, unemployment has more than doubled for men and women since 1980:

Numbers registered unemployed, by sex. Great Britain, 1976–85
Annual averages (in thousands)

	1976	1977	1978	1979	1980	1981	1982	1983	1984	1985
Male	969.1	1,004.0	965.7	887.2	1,129.1	1,773.3	2,055.9	2,133.5	2,109.6	2,165.3
Female	280.7	340.9	354.9	346.7	461.3	649.1	752.6	854.0	928.8	986.3
All persons	1,249.8	1,344.9	1,320.7	1,233.9	1,590.5	2,422.4	2,808.5	2,987.6	3,038.4	3,151.6

Equal Opportunities Commission, Ninth Annual Report, 1984

Predictably, it is unemployed men who are seen as the greater casualties:

Every time there is a report on television or in the papers we hear that because of unemployment boys are going to become disillusioned, alienated and violent and that's why we have to do something for the young.

Taking a letter   photo: Sally and Richard Greenhill

Computer terminal read-out   photo: Mike Abrahams/Network

Social Security office, London   photo: John Sturrock/Report

No one ever mentions *girls*. You would never know from the research community or the media that women are unemployed and that it's just as depressing, demoralizing and dire for women to be out of paid work as it is for men.

Dale Spender,
**There's Always Been
a Women's Movement
This Century**,
Pandora, 1983

New Ways

In all the gloom surrounding women's employment there are some chinks of light. Women are getting more confident in asserting themselves through work. Some fair-minded local authorities, companies and employers do now have 'positive action' policies. They actively encourage women to join training schemes, seek promotion and change managers' attitudes. They introduce viable alternatives to the traditional nine-to-five forty-hour week. They allow flexible working hours, which are as much appreciated by men as women. They implement job-sharing which opens up more interesting work to part-timers and maintains reasonable pay and conditions. A survey carried out by the Equal Opportunities Commission showed that sharers get paid the same hourly rate as for the comparable full-time job, benefit far more than part-timers from pension, sick pay, maternity leave and holiday schemes and feel more commitment to the job. The system of 'contract compliance' has also been successfully introduced by some city councils. Firms are not given contracts by the councils unless they can show that they observe good employment practices with regard to women, ethnic minorities and the disabled.

A new law with explosive potential for women was passed in 1984. It was an amendment to the Equal Opportunities Act of 1976, stipulating that within any company equal pay should be given for work of equal value. Hitherto the law said merely that equal pay should be given for equal work. As there is such acute job segregation not many women could be helped. And often wily managers would scramble working conditions so as to evade the law:

> After the Equal Pay Act I went through a shoe factory where they were making men's shoes and women's shoes. There were a lot of women pounding shoes – putting heels on actually. And there were a lot of men in another part putting heels on shoes. I said to the manager, 'I suppose you have equal pay?' And he said, 'Oh yes, we have equal pay.' So I asked him, 'Do you mean to say that the women here running this machine and the men over there running the same machine, get the same pay?' He said, 'Oh no, heavens no! Those men are putting heels on men's shoes. The women are putting heels on women's shoes. It's not the same work.' There were six nails going into each shoe and they were using the same machines. But the women didn't get the same pay.

Hazel Hunkins Hallinan,
quoted in Dale Spender,
**There's Always Been
a Women's Movement
This Century**,
Pandora, 1983

Since the Equal Value Amendment hundreds of women have made claims through their unions. A despatch office supervisor had her pay increased by more than £2,000 a year when her union argued that her work was of equal value to that covered by six grades occupied by men. A woman data processing clerk, working for a hosiery firm, got an increase of £55 a week by comparing her work with machine operators. This amendment could be used radically to alter the status of many 'women's jobs'. Hopefully women will put in the claims and argue their case.

Representation through a union is usually the crucial way of negotiating improvement at work. Increasing numbers of women now belong to trade unions – about 30 per cent of the total membership. The Women's Advisory Committee to the Trades Union Congress formulates negotiating demands for working women. The TUC has adopted a Charter for Working Women covering all aspects of their working lives – training, equal pay and opportunities, part-time work, job-sharing schemes, flexible working hours, child-care facilities, pension rights, social security, guidelines on sexual harassment at work, insurance and taxation rights. The policies at least are clear. It remains for them to be implemented.

Co-operatives, with shared responsibilities, shared decision-making and shared financial rewards, are another form of work structure which may benefit women. Women have spent enough years on the wrong side of the board-room door to appreciate the virtues of equitable management. Government and European Community schemes help co-ops start up and the Co-operative Development Agency in London acts as a clearing-house of information and advice. And more women, perhaps on the principle of 'if you can't join them, beat them', are now self-employed. There has been an increase in the past two years of 24 per cent in the number of small businesses run by women, though it is doubtful if many of these touch the true money supply.

Most hopeful of all has been the emergence of women's groups within professions and trades – groups for women in banking, computing, management, the media, medicine, publishing, and so on. These groups take their inspiration from and are part of the women's movement. They offer support, raise awareness, help individuals and put pressure on unions and management to change the systems that give women a raw deal.

Tea-break, lock factory, West Midlands
photo: Nick Hedges

Work systems are known to be unfair to women. There's legislation that makes discrimination illegal. There are enough government surveys, statistics and reports to fill libraries. There are campaigning groups on all aspects of women's work. There is recognition of the particular working needs of women – shared domestic responsibilities, flexible working hours, crèches. There is an acknowledgement that women are as able as men in virtually all areas of work and more able in many. There is acceptance that a woman's place is at work for most of her adult life. But if all the legislation and declared intentions are to be more than so much rhetoric, work systems have to be changed to accommodate women's interests too.

need more women in government

113

Model at trade fair   photo: Ulrike Preuss

6. 'BRIDES, MUMS AND SIZZLERS': IMAGE AND STEREOTYPING .

photo: Geoff Howard

Dressing up
photo: Sally and Richard Greenhill

There is a notion that children's books today should always show father (who is preferably an official in the Trade Union) washing up at the sink, while children of many colours and creeds play bisexual games in the garden, while Mama is underneath the car changing the gearbox.

Brian Alderson, children's book critic of **The Times**, opening the 1975 National Book League Exhibition

It is an appealing scenario, despite its satirical edge. But the speaker implies that opposition to sexual stereotyping in children's books will lead to formula writing and inhibit the creative talents of writers and illustrators. Puritanism is anathema to art, but there is no evidence to suggest that criticism on social grounds such as sexism is more damaging to talent than criticism on traditional literary and aesthetic grounds. Language and imagery reflect the prejudices of the society in which they evolve. English evolved in a white Anglo-Saxon patriarchal society. Unsurprisingly its vocabulary and grammar reflect attitudes that exclude or demean women. But women are now intent on exposing and eliminating those prejudices.

Notions of gender identity begin very early and it seems that most children's books are about boys. Even animal, machine and fantasy characters are usually male, and female and male characters are usually presented in stereotypical ways. Mother pig invariably wears the apron and father pig brings home, as it were, the bacon. Sharp-nosed research and analysis of sex stereotyping alerts people to the hidden persuasion, coercion and neglect of women and girls that examples and images in books create.

This year it would be different. I had a place now, an identity. I was Laurie Stratton, Gordon Ahearn's girl . . .

Lois Duncan, **Stranger with My Face**, Hamish Hamilton, 1983

In these words the teenage narrator defines her notion of herself as female. She has lost her will to the will of Gordon. It is femininity defined in terms of sexual plasticity. Someone has to be boss and it is he. Her expectations are zero-rated.

In 1980 a researcher, Geoffrey Walford, looked at physics textbooks used in schools and found that 80 per cent of illustrations showed only men, 8 per cent showed both sexes and only 12 per cent a woman or girl alone. These appeared in 'a bathing suit, in a bath, as a nurse, with a vacuum cleaner . . . much more often then they appear as active participants in experiments or a physics-related

116

production'. Commenting on how few girls take physics at school, he suggests that a change in 'image management' in physics textbooks could encourage them more.

In **Pour Out the Cocoa, Janet: Sexism in Children's Books** (Longman, 1983) Rosemary Stones analyses some of the manifestations of sexism in children's books, from covert bias to obvious stereotyping. She doesn't suggest that all sexist books – which may have other qualities – should be discarded, simply that parents and teachers help children to resist coercion. She asks a series of questions to do with work, exclusion, language, attitudes and activities, of which the following are a sample:

Schoolgirls
photo: Janine Wiedel

Are girls depicted as servants to boys?
' "Pour out the cocoa, Janet," said Peter, "and remember that we all like heaps of sugar." ' Enid Blyton, **Go Ahead Secret Seven**, most recent reprint, Knight, 1982.

Are girls excluded?
Rod Campbell's **ABC** (Abelard-Schuman, 1980) illustrates each letter of the alphabet with a picture of someone doing a job. Women only get five out of the 26 jobs.

Are the girls drawn smaller than the boys and associated with smaller objects?
'Jane has a little boat and Peter has a big boat . . .'
'Here they are with the horses. Jane likes her little horse . . . Peter has a big horse.' **Things We Do**, Ladybird Key Words, 4a, 1978.

Are girls presented as inferior or incapable?
'Jem quite enjoyed balancing on the metal rail. Susy stood and watched him with her hand to her mouth. Susy rarely did anything else when she was with him.' Doreen Roberts, **Jem in the Park**, OUP, 1975.

Does the resolution of the story depend on whether a girl is pretty or ugly?
'The king's daughter was bonny and good natured and everybody liked her. But the queen's daughter was ugly and ill-natured and nobody liked her.' Alan Garner, **The Three Golden Heads of the Well**, Collins, 1979.

Is male violence against women depicted as natural and normal?
'Then in the moonlight he beat her . . . he did it more coldly than in anger: she must learn, as all women must, that a man was her master, and that he, Dom, was that man.' John Christopher, **Dom and Va**, Hamish Hamilton, 1973.

Is it assumed that girls will be less adventurous and less able at games and technical jobs?
' "Let me have a turn with the scraper, Paul," she says. He gives it to her straight away though she won't be able to use it, he thinks, and he is right.' Jill Paton Walsh, **Goldengrove**, Macmillan, 1972.

Is marriage presented as the main goal and preoccupation in a girl's life?
' "Doesn't Mary Watson look beaut in that uniform!" said Beth. "I wouldn't mind being a policewoman myself, for a few years, before I get married." ' Noreen Shelley, **Faces in a Looking Glass**, OUP, 1974.

Books define acceptable and unacceptable behaviour for girls and boys, show the options available to them in society and the kinds of jobs appropriate for women and men. There is now a concerted effort by some authors, illustrators, editors and booksellers to depict girls and women in more complex, positive and diverse ways. The way women are depicted and coerced in advertising, the media, literature, professional, private and cultural life, is monitored, chronicled and commented on. The intention is to put the record straight.

Bit Parts

In the stories of childhood girls get the bit parts, and this goes on throughout their adult lives. It isn't necessary to stir from the living room to find examples of the extent of the neglect of women in the press and the media:

> A random check of two daily newspapers showed that out of 62 news items, 43 were about men, twelve were about women and men, four were about women and three weren't about human beings at all . . . Out of named individuals, 385 were men and 33 were women . . . The pattern remains typical of news coverage throughout the media especially in the 'serious' newspapers and on radio and television. A study of one local radio station, Radio Nottingham, found that men's voices occupy seven eighths of the two-and-a-half hour morning news programme. Women are featured more regularly in the 'popular' press, but these are almost invariably 'wives', 'mums', 'brides', 'mistresses', victims of crime or misfortune, TV stars or 'sizzlers' . . .
>
> A 1977 survey by the National Union of Journalists found that among 314 journalists employed on seven newspapers in the north of England 279 were men and 35 were women. All editors and deputies were male; all sports specialists were male, all photographers but one were male; there were 69 male and 11 female sub-editors, 42 male and eight female features/specialist writers and 99 male and 23 female reporters. That pattern has changed very little – nor is it substantially different in other parts of the country.

Anna Coote and
Beatrix Campbell,
Sweet Freedom,
Picador, 1982

People like Margaret Thatcher, the Princess of Wales and the Queen Mother get saturation coverage, but usually women featuring in the news are attached to – generally married to – some newsworthy man. They are almost entirely absent from the sports, business and financial pages. Men's football, cricket and takeover bids are the games of our time and the results are broadcast to women on the international news.

If you flip through the four TV channels, chances are that images of men will appear on the screen. On radio panel games, chat shows and arts programmes, women are invariably outnumbered by three to one. Such unequal representation leaves the lone woman unsupported, makes gender intellectually conspicuous and means that she has to contend with more patronizing or hostile and difficult dynamics than might exist were the balance more equal. It would be interesting to hear a few such programmes with a token man.

Feminists are generally described by their opponents as 'shrill'

118

or 'strident', depicted as cutting their hair with the kitchen scissors and derided for their physical unattractiveness and their neglect of true 'womanliness'. The satirical magazine **Private Eye** runs a column called 'Wimmin'. 'All loony feminist nonsense gratefully received,' it advertises. '£5 paid for entries printed.' The line illustration to the column shows four breastless, odd-looking women with knives poised, about to castrate a bound, semi-clad man. The image was first suggested by Freud:

When the little girl discovers her own deficiency, from seeing a male genital, it is only with hesitation and reluctance that she accepts the unwelcome knowledge. She clings obstinately to the expectation of one day having a genital of the same kind too and her wish of it survives long after her hope has expired. The child invariably regards castration in the first instance as a misfortune peculiar to herself. Only later does she realize that it extends to certain other children and lastly to certain grown-ups. When she comes to understand the general nature of this characteristic, it follows that femaleness – and with it, of course, her mother – suffers a great depreciation in her eyes.

Sigmund Freud,
Female Sexuality, 1931

Worse follows:

The wish to get the longed-for penis eventually in spite of everything may contribute to the motives that drive a mature woman to analysis, and what she may reasonably expect from analysis – a capacity for instance to carry on an intellectual profession – may often be recognized as a sublimated modification of this repressed wish.

photo: Ged Murray

Sigmund Freud was bad news for women's liberation. He came on to the intellectual scene just when women were finding the courage to challenge their social and economic dependency. They were struggling for the right to learn and work and share in the capitalist system which men claimed as their natural prerogative. Then Freud arrived with his theories of penis envy, castration complex and innate sexual inferiority. The more lurid of his ideas got taken out of context and used as a justification of patriarchy. However tentative or open to debate he might have meant them to be, they were received as if they had the force of special insight. This was what people were really like, their true being; the rest was surface show. Would-be emancipated women froze in their tracks. It wasn't that they wanted the learning, the self-expression and the professions assiduously denied them for so long. What they really wanted was penises. It was a formula that devalued their efforts as effectively as any legislation:

Of all the factors that have served to perpetuate a male-orientated society, that have hindered the free development of women as human beings in the Western world today, the emergence of Freudian analysis has been the most serious . . . Any woman who fails to achieve orgasm on occasion, who discovers that she does not love her husband as much as she feels she ought, or who finds that she does not want to start a family, or is not as involved with her children as society tells her she should be, is liable to worry about whether she is in some way rejecting her own femininity.

Eva Figes,
Patriarchal Attitudes,
Virago, 1978

It took an irreverent Australian woman, Germaine Greer, to

Ladies' hairdresser, Lancashire photo: Daniel Meadows

THIS FIRM
HIRES ONLY
SLAVE LABOUR

blow Freud's po-faced theories sky high forty years later in **The Female Eunuch**. Since the seventies women have been extremely eloquent in describing, defining and claiming their own sexuality. No male politician, religious leader or sexologist will again succeed in telling them what they really feel, or what they should really do. More than ever before women are making their own decisions about their own bodies and feelings. They claim equal respect for a range of sexual convictions: free love, caution, celibacy, serial monogamous heterosexuality, marriage, sequential marriage, open marriage, bisexuality or lesbianism, lesbian feminism, lesbian separatism, a good book and an early night – whatever suits, or seems like a good idea at the time or for the long term. Sexual freedom and assertiveness, the right to choose and not be coerced into any particular sexual role, control of unwanted conception through contraception and unwanted pregnancy through abortion, are landmarks of liberation for women.

Of all the things women want – pay parity, equal work opportunities, equal political representation, crèches, maternity leave, pension rights and so on – penises are not on the list. Women do not want to be men, any more than black people want to be white. The problem for women, which they are now intent on solving, is to establish who they are in terms of an expressed common identity, when they have been told so forcefully and for so long what they are not.

rather her want boobs

As well as Freudians, the 'moral right' make concerted attempts to limit women in the name of God and the past. Their attacks tend to be ritualistic, intellectually woolly and rooted in the idea of the superiority of men. There is much talk of the 'sanctity of marriage' on matters of divorce and the 'sanctity of life' on matters of abortion, and very little empathy with the needs and circumstances of each individual woman or girl. 'East of Suez everyone knows what I'm talking about,' the pulp novelist Barbara Cartland said in a Radio 4 interview. Apparently her books sell well there. She advocates complete double standards for men and women, describes young women who have 'lost their virginity' as 'shop-soiled', implying that no honourable man would 'want them', says that women should not be MPs and talks of 'sexual submission' and 'good wives'. She also admits to not liking women much and thinking them stupid. East of Suez many women are subjected to clitoridectomies and infibulation, must cover their faces and live in purdah, and are denied rights of citizenship.

Man-Made Language

The 'female eunuch' syndrome extends to everyday language too:

Only recently have we become aware that conventional English usage, including the generic use of masculine-gender words, often obscures the actions, the contributions and sometimes the very presence of women. Turning our backs on that insight is an option, of course, but it is an option like teaching children that the world is flat.

Casey Miller and Kate Swift, **The Handbook of Non-Sexist Writing for Writers, Editors and Speakers**, The Women's Press, 1981

Efforts to make language less denying of women are decried or ignored by those who seek to preserve the status quo. The argument seems vaguely to be that the spirit of Shakespeare will be desecrated if words like 'chairman', 'spokesman' and 'he' are modified when applied to women too. Objections to the changes are beginning to sound decidedly old hat. Even the Civil Service now has guidelines for non-sexist writing, as do unions, journalists and copy editors. Clause 10 of the National Union of Journalists Code of Conduct says:

> A journalist shall only mention a person's race, colour, creed, illegitimacy, marital status (or lack of it), gender or sexual orientation if this information is strictly relevant. A journalist shall neither originate nor process material which encourages discrimination on any of the above-mentioned grounds.

Even people of far from radical disposition, like bank managers, undertakers and some solicitors, can now sometimes be persuaded to use the social title 'Ms', a concession to the feminist view that

> When you call me Miss or Mrs
> You invade my private life
> For it's not the public's business
> If I am, or was, a wife.

The mould is getting chipped, if not broken.

Women's beauty, breasts, eyes, hair and gentleness are the stuff of many odes. The moon is, or was female, as are ships, boats, cars and things that get ridden, driven, broken up and sold for spares. Overall the language is startlingly disparaging towards the female sex. Women are called bitches, cows, shrews and fishwives in a very different tone from the way men might be referred to as dogs, bulls, voles or fishhusbands. The **Penguin Dictionary of Proverbs** has 73 entries under 'Wisdom', all of which refer to men. There is no category called 'Men', the assumption being, presumably, that they are the fount of all adage. Under 'Women' there are 104 references sub-sectioned into their dissimulation, tears, wilfulness, garrulousness, capriciousness, impulsiveness, stupidity and greed.

Changes in language usually occur imperceptibly, but some take place with intended speed. Such was the case in the 1960s when 'black' replaced 'Negro'.

> A few short years ago, if you called most Negroes 'blacks', it was tantamount to calling us niggers. But now black is beautiful and black is proud. There are relatively few people, white or black, who do not recognize what has happened. Black people have freed themselves from the dead weight of albatross blackness that once hung around their necks. They have done it by picking it up in their arms and holding it out with pride for all the world to see . . .

US Congresswoman Shirley Chisholm

The language is littered with the carcasses of a flock of albatrosses as far as women are concerned. For centuries the word 'man' has been used in ways that obscure women's contribution to civilization. The list is endless of books and programmes with titles like **The Family of Man**, **The Ascent of Man**, **The Condition of Man**, **The Identity of Man**, **The Mind of Man**, **Man the Hunter**, **Man the Scientist**, **Man the Artist**, **Man the Lifeboat**. The abandoning of 'man' as a false generic is extremely useful to women. 'The Family of Man' is really 'The Human

photo: Jill Posener

122

Monday Club ball
photo: Homer Sykes

Family'. More and more people are saying 'men and women', 'he or she', when they mean just that. It has become conspicuous how people choose to use gender in language. Some carry on obliviously. They seem rather quaint. Some stick to the old style, aware of the arguments and feelings, but scathing and dismissive of these. They seem rather horrid. And an increasing number of people stumble their way into self-revision to make the language be seen to include women too. Every time this happens it is like a nudge to memory – that women are entitled to equal rights.

Perhaps some linguistic purists refer to disappearing down personholes, find sexist offence where it is hard to construe and seize on sexist slips as proof of hard-core prejudice. But even if vestiges of bias survive, it is proving perfectly possible to revise the language to include women, without any grave renunciation of eloquence, grace or style.

Casey Miller and Kate Swift explain how

photo: Jill Furmanovsky

People come up with all sorts of reasons why in word pairs males almost always come first: 'men and women', 'male and female', 'his and hers', 'boys and girls', 'guys and dolls' and so on. Some linguists theorize that it is easier to say a single-syllable word like men than a two-syllable word like women, and that we tend to put the single syllable first as a result. Another theory is that the order has something to do with prosodic patterns: since men and women and male and female scan as two trochees, they trip more lightly off the tongue than they would if reversed to scan as a trochee and an iamb. Neither theory accounts for 'husbands and wives' or

123

such other familiar phrases as 'coffee and cake', 'needle and thread', 'hammer and tongs', 'fathers and sons', or – to get to the root of the matter – 'Adam and Eve' . . .

. . . Those who have no stake in maintaining the so-called natural order of the sexes do not set one before the other as a matter of rule; they allow, instead, for variations that come naturally.

Whatever you or he might think, change is under way.

If women dislike being called men, they also dislike being called girls. In the days of Empire, not long past, adult Indian and African men were called 'boy' by the sahibs and memsahibs who paid their paltry wages. 'I'll have my girl run off a dozen copies', 'Ask one of the girls to find it', are everyday phrases in offices. They refer to adult women. They are as patronizing and demeaning as their racist equivalent. 'Career girl' is a snide term that belittles achievement, and pleasantries like 'what are you girls drinking?' can irritate women who are well out of their teens.

Another way of diminishing women is by referring to their sex when the issues are, or should be, training, experience, talent and achievement: 'lady' is a quite gratuitous adjective in 'lady barrister wins case'. It is only marginally less offensive than the aberration of referring to women, no matter how successful, as appendages of their husbands or domestic circumstances, or by their physical characteristics, when men would be described by their business or other achievements: 'General Ponsonby's slim, attractive daughter, Anthea, won the Croxley chess tournament . . .' – that sort of thing is all too common.

Advertising Women

Language is used to demean women and make them invisible. Advertising turns them into objects and chops them up in pieces. Images of semi-clad women, or bits of them, are used to sell everything: sacks of potatoes, cars, videos, diamonds, dictation machines, lawnmowers, washing machines, underwear, cosmetics, stockings and the rest:

> No city in the world boasts such a density of sexual objectification on its billboards and subway ads as does London.

Juliet Mitchell, **Women's Estate**, Penguin, 1971

The images show women packaged, brand new and ready for consumption like the things they are used to advertise. Their hands sell custard powder and diamond rings, their smiles sell washing powder and fast cars, their legs and breasts sell alcohol and farm implements:

still – more domestic than 'glam'!

> The connection between women and domestic happiness, women and glamour, women and sexuality, means that images of women are used to evoke these qualities in advertising any product, whether it is a car, a cigarette, or a lawnmower. In advertising women are like a currency that can be used to buy or sell anything. In adverts women become interchangeable with the products they are selling, often they even become part of the product, or are shown contained in it. Images of women are, in reality, products that are bought and sold by advertisers; and in these images women themselves function as just another product on the market.

Judith Williamson, 'Women and Advertising', British Council article, 1984

Underground station, London   photo: Francis Glibbery

Chelsea fashion show   photo: Jill Furmanovsky

An image of a slim, blonde, naked woman is shown curled *inside* a pomander, along with the vials of cologne, powder, soap and bath oil her nakedness is being used to sell. She and the products are one and the same thing. 'Everybody needs love. Fabergé made love and called it Kiku,' runs the legend.

Hairdresser
photo: Ulrike Preuss

The proposition of much advertising is that love, in the shape of a man, is the goal in every woman's life and the way to score that goal is by being physically perfect, a beauty queen. Advertisements continually make women aware of their alleged imperfections, then offer to sell them solutions to their supposed problems through slimming foods, skin creams, shampoos, deodorants, depilatories and so on. Adolescent girls and young women make themselves ill with worry over whether they are too fat, their hips too big, their breasts too small, their bodies hairy or their legs the wrong shape. Women are aware of being constantly looked at and sexually assessed. They are encouraged by advertisers to be perpetually anxious as to whether they are wearing the right clothes, make-up or perfume.

Notions of 'looking pretty' are impressed on girls from a very early age. They become a crucial way of getting adult approval. In a study of adolescent girls at school, the most popular 'ideal' jobs aspired to were those of model or hairdresser. (Except for a few high-flying stylists, hairdressing is among the worst paid of women's occupations.) Looks are focused on obsessively as the key to women's

**Dressing up
for a wedding, Northumberlan**
photo: Karen Melvin

"We talked all evening; suddenly he noticed my lips and leaned towards me... I knew my lips still looked tempting, my lipstick didn't even need a nervous lick." New Outdoor Girl Lipsticks. Long Lasting Cream, Pearl & Super Moist Gloss. Thirty fabulous shades with a brand new formula, shape and stylish marbled case.

Outdoor Girl
Cosmetics that work-beautifully

value, and other abilities and skills get underrated. This is not to minimize the value of looking good. But self-confidence and self-fulfilment are the best basic ingredients of appearance – they shine through the pan-stick. And advertisers, in their cunning to create consumers, attack both these aspects of feminine identity, then imply that they are to be gained in a spurious way.

The perfect woman of the advertising hoardings is an object, any piece of which must itself be perfect:

Women's bodies have become fragmented in advertising as products multiply, as manufacturers seek new areas to colonize. Each part of the body on its own comes to stand for femininity: a shaved leg, a mascarad eye.*   *Judith Williamson, ibid.

The transsexual April Ashley was, after paying for an operation in Casablanca, one of *Vogue*'s favourite models for underwear. Images of bits of her were also used to advertise deodorants and heated hair rollers. It is difficult to believe in the perfect female armpit, leg, waist or profile, if it might equally well belong to a man.

In advertising images women's bodies are used to represent every aspect of a constructed perfection. This is because 80 per cent of all shopping in Britain is done by women. They are the conspicuous spenders, the crucial market. Advertisers devise and exploit images of 'female identity' – all of which supposedly need satisfying by some product. The main image is that of ideal mother and housewife. There are ads galore of mother dotingly serving her husband and children. If she is helped by anyone it is her daughter, who is growing up to be just like her:

The hand that rocks the cradle, loads the washing machine, whips up a soufflé and knits a jumper is never male. Only occasionally is the hand gripping a saw, stripping down the car, or clipping a hedge, a woman's.   Cynthia White, 'Women's Magazines', British Council article, 1984

These same hands must never look as if they've done a day's work in their lives. They must be unblemished, with painted nails and adorned with rings. For they also belong to the lover, mistress and wife of a man and reflect his earning power and therefore importance:

Hands. Seen almost as soon as your face. On show. Touching. Holding. Loving. Nail polish is as important as make-up. That's why we call Cutex the make-up for nails.

Woman the wife and homemaker, or bits of her, must also represent all aspects of personal life – love, sex, romance, mystery. Home, which is a woman, is shown as a haven from the world of 'men's work'. But woman also provides all the freedom, excitement and wildness missing from business life:

For those of you who have been civilized long enough . . . In contrast to all the civilized world's polite perfumes we bring you Wild Musk. The most sensual, frankly arousing fragrance ever unleashed.

The fact that women do paid work outside the home is scarcely ever reflected. However, since the Women's Movement advertising has cashed in on the image of the 'liberated woman'. Single working women provide new markets in

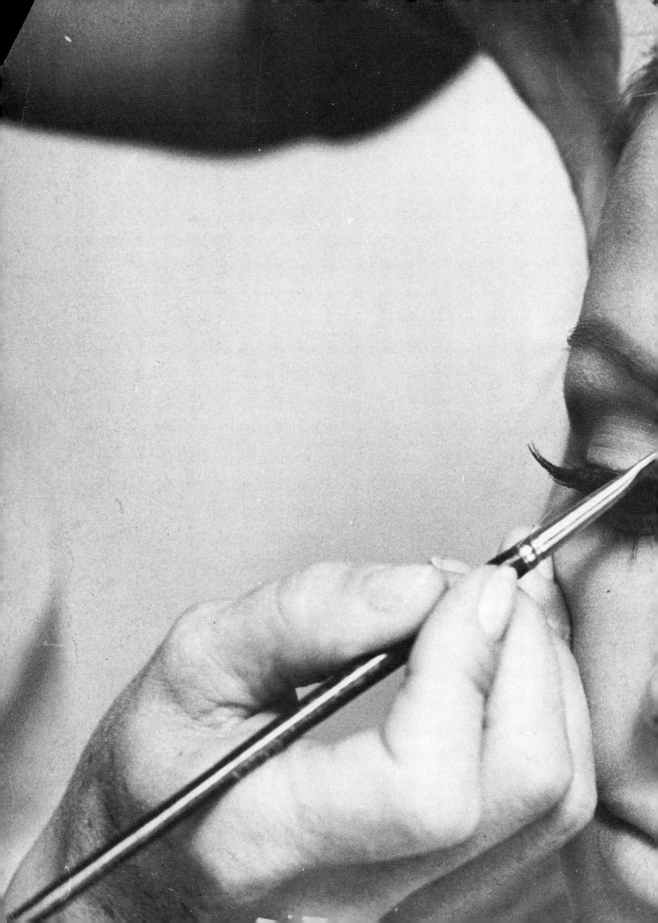

areas that used to be dominated by men, such as insurance, cars and stereos. Yet for women, work, like sexual attractiveness, is for the most part depicted as a series of problems – about make-up, deodorants, chipped nail polish, period pains, tampons and so on:

> If ever an anti-perspirant had to work it was today! And it did! Soft and Gentle kept me dry all right . . . I was a bit sceptical when I found it didn't sting even after you've shaved. But it really kept me cool and dry. I mean, I got the job didn't I!

Imagine her job prospects had she used a different deodorant or not shaved her armpits.

Women's magazines are another massive industry: **Woman**, **Woman's Own**, **Woman's Realm**, **Woman's World**. Their content heavily favours the twin themes of domesticity and sexual attractiveness. Marriage and the home are women's pre-eminent social destiny and the way they look, cook, clean the clothes and smell is what gets them there and keeps them there. As with advertising, although some magazines present a more progressive, socially involved picture, most reinforce the home-centred, sex-object myth.

Stereotypes of femininity polarize women and perpetuate their inequalities. They steer them away from wider opportunities and circumscribe their lives. They reinforce prejudice and bar progress. The damage of stereotyping was described in the government White Paper **Equality for Women** which provided the basis for the Sex Discrimination Act of 1976:

Beauty care evening, Lancashire
photo: Daniel Meadows

Beyond the basic physiological differences between men and women lies a whole range of differences between individual men and individual women in all aspects of human ability. The differences within each sex far outweigh the differences between the sexes. But there is insufficient recognition that the variations of character and ability within each sex are greater and more significant than the differences between the sexes. Women are often treated as unequal because they are alleged to be inferior to men in certain respects and the consequences of their unequal treatment are then seen as evidence of their inferiority . . . Many who make the important decisions about the treatment of women do not discriminate against them because of conscious personal prejudice, but because of prejudices of which they are unaware, or the prejudices (real or assumed) which they ascribe to others – management, employees, customers or colleagues.

The unequal status of women is wasteful of the potential talents of half our population . . .

Since the seventies women have retaliated against the way they are portrayed in advertising, the media, books and language. This retaliation ranges from scrupulous, thoroughly researched analyses to the laconic editing of a couple of words sprayed on a particularly sexist ad. Books, articles and organizations like the Women's Monitoring Network of Sexism in the Media expose the cynicism with which images of women are used as commercial barter. Manufacturers and the media, however, generally ignore the challenge to change their ways. Advertising, trashy TV soap operas and newspapers unrelentingly present simplistic, 'idealized', artificial images of women to such an extent that these are far more in circulation than the complex, diverse, often more or less androgynous picture of what might perhaps be true.

Disco, Wolverhampton
photo: Chris Steele-Perkins

I AM HERE
FOR THESE

MY 6 GRAND CHILDREN

MY FORMER
PUPILS

7.

THE QUIET REVOLUTION: PROTEST AND CHANGE.

Textile workers, Manchester
photo: Sally and Richard Greenhill

Nurses
photo: Laurie Sparham/Report

It is only when women start to organize in large numbers that we become a political force and begin to move towards the possibility of a truly democratic society . . .

Sheila Rowbotham,
**Women, Resistance
and Revolution**,
Allan Lane, 1972;
Penguin 1974

Parallel to the intricately related worlds of power politics and big business from which women are, for the most part, rudely excluded, is a world of organizational activity which excludes men. There is a grass-roots reappraisal of women's social and political role, a consciousness and determination that women's place in society will no longer be ignored. There are now hundreds of national women's organizations, most of which have regional representation. Many began out of radical opposition to 'man-made' society that neglects and discourages women's interests and needs. Many started up with the renaissance of the women's movement in the seventies. Groups of long standing revised themselves at that time and drew fresh breath. Nor, despite the glumness, discouragement and political barbarism of the eighties, have they gone away. Far from it. More women's projects and ventures start up weekly. Women's events are packed out, be they discussions, theatre groups, discos, or whatever. Groups are not modelled on the old authoritarian lines with chains of command, but structured on principles of equality. There is no overall organizational network linking them. Many work as specific interest groups. All have some consciousness of being part of a broader movement of social change and will support in varying degree what other groups are doing. They sting and deflate the leviathan with increasing frequency.

Activity now flourishes in all areas of concern to women: work, pay and welfare benefits; education opportunities; racial equality; sexual freedom and reproductive rights; sexual harassment and violence; the peace campaign; women's health, and so on. There is pressure for better political and trade-union organization, for ordination into the church, for realistic portrayal in the media, for an end to sex discrimination in sport and the arts. Organizations mushroom despite lack of financial or moral support from central government and even hostility to them. Women have also organized information centres to co-ordinate and disseminate news about campaigns and groups.

The Women's Research and Resources Centre, for example, loans books and journals and keeps a research index on all aspects of women's studies.

The Fawcett Society, which assembled Britain's largest feminist library, campaigns on equality issues and for greater involvement of women in public life. Rights of Women (ROW), works as a pressure group to achieve legislation which benefits women. Women and Manual Trades is a campaigning and support network of women working and training in traditionally male jobs like plumbing and carpentry. Women in Banking encourages women to apply for executive and managerial positions. Women in Industry, Women in Management, Women in Publishing, Women in Telecom, Women in the Civil Service, all promote the status of women in these careers. The Academic Women's Achievement Group looks for ways of ending the under-representation of women in university work. The Cinema of Women, and businesses like it, seek out and distribute films by and about women. The Women's Aid Federation provides refuges for women and their children who are victims of domestic violence. Rape Crisis Centres provide 24-hour phone services offering support and advice to assaulted women. Women Against Violence Against Women (WAVAW) campaigns against pornography and violence to women and calls for appropriate sentencing of sex offenders. Gingerbread and the National Council for One Parent Families help single people – most of whom are women – with children. The National Abortion Campaign (NAC) campaigns for free abortion on demand and adequate provision of National Health Service outpatient abortion clinics. The Women's Therapy centre offers a counselling and referral service. The Women's Committee of the Trades Union Congress does detailed research and campaigns on charters of equality

Women Against Violence Against Women
photo: Derek Speirs/Report

Refuge for battered women   photo: Markéta Luskacová

and fairness for working women, covering collective bargaining, anti-racism, child-care facilities, positive action programmes, health risks, sexual harassment, low pay, welfare benefits, training schemes and so on. Local black women's groups campaign against racist nationality laws and defend women who are harassed and discriminated against when they attempt to get essential services. Neighbourhood women's 'consciousness-raising' groups have been flourishing since the late sixties. 'A Woman's Place' library maintains an index of women's groups. The Women's National Commission, an advisory committee to the government, produces lists of national women's organizations in Great Britain. There are about 200 detailed entries. What the government makes of the information is unclear.

Books and Courses

Underpinning all this activity and giving it intellectual cohesion, are the women's studies courses organized over the past ten years. Most universities, polytechnics and adult education institutes and many schools now offer such courses. And they filter through into the NOW and the WOW and the New Horizons, Fresh Start and Return to Work women's adult education and training schemes. The women's studies courses are generally accepted by the establishment world of higher education, though they are essentially anti-establishment, challenging traditional notions of women and a woman's place. They are organized by and for women. Interpretations of the world and its history are made through women's eyes instead of men's.

> Just as organized feminism breaks the silence and opens women's mouths on the matter of their supposed contentment, so women's studies asks, repetitively, where are the women and why are their voices not heard? Women are not absent from history, or art, or society, or whatever; they are present in distorted and distorting images, and mammoth archaeological expeditions are required to bring the reality of their existence to our attention.

Ann Oakley,
Subject Women,
Fontana, 1982

The women's studies courses range wide: women and art; women and literature; women in history; women's health; the sexual politics of work; women and education; women in society; sex stereotyping in secondary-school subjects; the sociology of domestic economy; women and the law; women and social policy; women, class and power; women and property; women as property; and many more. And with the groups and courses go the journals, the abstracts and the newsletters, the publishing houses and the bookshops, the archives and the libraries. A massive network is being constructed to make women visible, change the old definitions, shape new confidence and defend women from the repeat of past wrongs.

The Frankfurt Book Fair, the big annual book sales bonanza for publishers worldwide, gives evidence of the popularity of books on women's studies and women's issues. Sales are on a par with books on cookery and crime. The first of the women's publishing houses, Virago, was founded in 1972 in reaction to the historic 'male control' of publishing with its concomitant neglect of women's writing. Initially

EVERY CHILD A WANTED CHILD

Virago had an arrangement with an established publisher for production and distribution of its books. They were successful enough by 1977 to be entirely independent, and became profitable enough to join a group of three other major publishers in 1982. They specialize in the reissue of books by women left out of print, and publish books on feminist theory and new fiction by women from various countries.

Peace

On matters of war and peace the gap between protesters and policy-makers has never been wider. United States cruise missiles are installed in this country despite one of the largest public protests ever. Women are in the forefront of the campaign for peace. Perhaps they are quicker than men to see through jingoism to the suffering of war. The 'Greenham Factor' has been a testimony to the power of women to orchestrate sensational, imaginative, yet non-violent protest. Thousands of women focused world attention on women's opposition to the nuclear threat.

The women's peace camp began after the government announced that 96 American cruise missiles were to be sited at the US base at Greenham Common, Berkshire. Cruise apparently flies close to the ground avoiding normal radar. It contains a computer with a map of Europe and Russia imprinted on its memory. Once launched, each missile can reach its target with the destructive force of 15 Hiroshima bombs.

On 28 August 1981, 40 women set out on a protest walk from Wales to Greenham Common. When they got there they decided to stay and try to obstruct and prevent the arrival of the missiles. Their camp grew to thousands. When the local council forbade the women to put up tents or park caravans, they slept under plastic sheeting. Demonstrations drew in many more not camping full time at Greenham. On 12 December 1982, 30,000 women, holding hands, encircled the nine-mile perimeter fence of the future nuclear weapons base. They decorated the fence with children's clothing, family photographs, posters, candles, 'personal affirmations of life'. The next day 3,000 women lay in the road, blocking the entrances of the base to stop the construction work going on there. The campaigners issued statements about their aims and methods:

> We are ordinary women who feel that nothing is more important in our lives than preventing nuclear holocaust. For years politicians have been talking about arms negotiations and people have been demonstrating with marches, but not one nuclear weapon has been stopped. We choose non-violence because we believe we cannot counter violence with violence, that we must use other methods of solving our differences if we are to survive as a species.
>
> There are no leaders at the women's peace camp, no formal organization, no hierarchy. The camp at Greenham is a focus for us. Some women live there all the time, some visit for a day and then take back their ideas to their own areas and encourage other women to act. We feel that every one of us must take personal responsibility for what the government is doing, supposedly in our name.

Greenham Common
Women's Peace Camp,
1983

142

Obstructing building works at Greenham Common photo: Homer Sykes

photo: Ed Barber

Greenham campaigner   photo: Homer Sykes

Arrest for obstruction   photo: Ed Barber

The women staged symbolic 'die-ins'. They scaled the camp fence and danced on the silos built to house the missiles. They got arrested, fined, evicted and stoned. They painted peace symbols on US war planes. They cut the wire of the fence. The Minister of Defence warned that they risked being shot. At no point were they provoked into violence. On 17 November 1983 the missiles arrived. The women formed a blockade; 117 were arrested. On 11 December 50,000 women encircled the base and pulled part of the fencing down. There were hundreds of arrests, mostly for 'breach of the peace'. The women's reply was that it is a breach of the peace to have these weapons on the Common.

Cruise missiles are in the silos. In the short term the women failed in their objectives but their style of protest is inspirational. They brought together different strands of the women's peace movement: women in the Campaign for Nuclear Disarmament (CND), the Women's Peace Alliance (WPA), Women Opposed to the Nuclear Threat (WONT). In 1981 another camp was set up at Molesworth in Cambridgeshire by women in the Fellowship of Reconciliation, a Christian group committed to non-violence.

The Greenham women cut through the euphemistic rhetoric of the Ministry of Defence. They voiced equal concern with the lives of Russian women and children. And their views are shared by the majority of British people, who oppose the siting of American missiles in this country and a budget that spends more on the apparatus of war than on education.

Events at Greenham showed the world how women can organize on a large scale and become a political force. Less publicized have been the campaign by women for a non-violent solution to the strife in Northern Ireland, the protest by women over sackings in the printing industry concomitant with the sudden introduction of new technology, and the part played by women in the miners' strike of 1984–5. The protracted strike was sustained to defend not only men's jobs, but the existence of whole communities. Central to it was the contribution made by the wives of miners and women's action groups throughout the country. Women picketed the pits, raised funds, ran soup kitchens, organized food parcels for striking miners and their families, addressed meetings, rallied support and put up with hardship and hostility in defence of mining families' right to a decent life.

Irish women in London
photo: Nick Oakes

Protest against pit closures
photo: Jenny Matthews/Format

Belfast, 1978 photo: Chris Steele-Perkins

Violence

Another area of direct action is in protest against social violence towards women. The historic silence – born of depression, guilt and fear – from victims of rape, incest and sexual assault and harassment, has now been broken. Women are encouraged to speak of their ordeals to organizations which offer support and legal advice. There are now 26 Rape Crisis Centres in cities and towns, offering a 24-hour phone service, support, advice and a counsellor to go to the police station with assaulted women. Recommendations have been submitted to the Criminal Law Revision Committee, advising changes to the Sexual Offences Act. Guidelines have been issued to the police on their treatment of women victims of sex assault. An Incest Survivors' Group has been set up. Women trade unionists are demanding that the whole union movement tackles the problem of sexual harassment of women at work. Twenty-five per cent of all violent crimes are domestic. There are 150 Women's Aid refuges offering free temporary accommodation to women and children who are afraid to go home because of the violence of the men with whom they live.

Women Against Violence Against Women (WAVAW) is a national campaigning network. It supports direct action against sex shops, pornography and video nasties. A Leeds group called 'Angry Women' have so far set fire to three sex shops. Their press release states:

> We are protesting and fighting back against images portraying women as sexual conveniences for men to abuse, hurt and degrade. Pornography in

Strip club
photo: David Hurn/Hillelson

films, magazines and sex shops incites men to treat women as instruments solely for their use. Porn is big money-making business based on the suffering of women.

Leeds Women's Liberation Newsletter, April 1981

Many schools, councils and local groups run courses in self-defence. WAVAW and other women's groups issue guidelines on avoidance of attack from strangers in the street. Individual court cases cause a stir – a judge stated in 1982 that a woman hitch-hiking at night was guilty of 'contributory negligence' when a man offered her a lift and then raped her. Groups of women, either collectively or with local authority help have set up collectively run late-night transport or taxi services for women. Women want the freedom of the streets and to scotch the notion of themselves as victims or fair game.

'The Right to Choose'

Women now speak out publicly about their sexuality in a way that would not formerly have been possible. Sex, the law and a prescriptive moral tone have made a lot of people miserable down the years. In an unprecedented way women are sloughing off the confused expectations and repressions of the past and staking a claim to their own desires. Which leads, of course, to a variety of behaviour, some of it discomfiting to those of settled views.

Despite the wishes of petitioners and politicians, the age of consent and the age of puberty refuse to synchronize. It is illegal for a man over 14 to have sexual intercourse with a woman under 16. It is only he who can be prosecuted, as the law considers it irrelevant whether she chose to have sex or not. She can, though, be placed in care on the grounds that she is in 'moral danger' because of her 'abnormal sexual appetite'.

Whether it is advisable or not, 20 per cent of young women under 16 are sexually active. The National Council for One Parent Families, searching for a more sympathetic and pragmatic approach, calls for the abolition of the age-of-consent laws. As one young woman put it:

We as young women get the worst of it all round. Some doctors won't give contraception to women under sixteen and a lot of young women are frightened to go and obtain contraception or to tell a doctor they are pregnant in case the doctor tells their parents.

I believe that all women should have the right to abortion on demand, free contraception and we should be able to get info. on these things at any age.

I'm not saying that we should all be having sex before we are sixteen. What I am saying is that at the moment the law decides when we should have sex not us, the law says when we should get contraception not us, the law says whether we can have an abortion not us. We should not have our sexual relationships made illegal and should not be punished for them.

Quoted in
Shocking Pink, No. 1

Whatever the law, the concerns of women working in the relevant advice services – the Pregnancy Advisory Service, National Council for One Parent Families, Gingerbread, Family Planning Association, British Pregnancy

Advisory Service and local youth counselling agencies – are to offer immediate practical and supportive help to the young women who come through their doors.

Whether you are 16 or 60, lesbianism has never been illegal. Victorian legislators introduced vicious penal measures against male homosexuals, but women unaroused by men were assumed to be asexual, so there was little point in outlawing what could not occur. Passionate friendships between women were known to exist, but these were not thought to have a sexual edge. Homosexuality for men is now legal if both consent and are over 21 – despite the fact that many gay men know their identity years before that magic age. For women, silence is thought best.

Silence about lesbianism has not of course meant acceptance, approval or even tolerance. The common social experience for lesbians, outside the milieu of friends and lovers, has been ridicule, prejudice and exclusion: ostracized by their families, unsupported if in difficulty or bereaved, victimized at work or over child custody or housing rights. From the seventies on, lesbians have broken silence, published literature about lesbianism, talked openly of their experiences, set up support structures, clubs and meeting places and sought an end to discrimination against them at work, in housing, in social situations and in the prejudice of the law. The success of the lesbian and gay liberation movements has been to give homosexual people a context to be positive about themselves and open about their identity. Some women see their lesbianism as political – the ultimate resistance of coercion to step into prescribed roles, a refusal to fulfil the male image of womanhood or to concede to male superiority. Certainly, if viewed politically, lesbianism is the extreme challenge to orthodox notions of a woman's place.

'A Woman's Right to Choose' is the central issue behind campaigns for safe, reliable contraception, backed up by safe abortion. Without the right to control their bodies, women cannot control their destinies. The 1967 Abortion Act legalized abortions under certain conditions, but their availability on the National Health Service varies throughout the country, depending on local facilities and attitudes. In Northern Ireland abortion remains illegal except in extreme circumstances. The National Abortion Campaign seeks to extend a woman's right to choose:

> There is an entire climate which promotes certain women having babies and which does not favour others, on the basis of prejudice and oppression to do with colour, class, marital status, sexual preference, disability and notions of the 'fit/unfit' mother. We come up against these notions when we go for contraception, if we need an abortion, if we want artificial insemination by donor, if sterilization is an option, if we need tests for infertility, or if we are pregnant or want to get pregnant. We come up against them precisely at the point where we attempt to make whatever limited choices are open to us, given our individual circumstances.

National Abortion Campaign, in **Outwrite**, September 1983

Women are campaigning against cuts in the health service which threaten special health services and clinics for women, including women's hospitals.

The 'Right to Choose' campaign extends beyond reproduction to a rejection of the idea that men are necessarily the experts on women's health and well-being. Women have organized self-help activities around health issues. These look beyond purely medical solutions to health problems. There are 'well woman' clinics and self-help groups centred on issues such as anorexia, compulsive eating, isolation as mothers. More than twice as many women as men consult their doctors with emotional problems. Women's Therapy Centres work with individuals and groups on mental health issues. They see women's mental health in relation to their role in society and are critical of treatment which does nothing to alleviate the causes of anxiety and depression, but simply blankets symptoms with pills. The Women's Health Information Centre disseminates information on women's health, a black women's health centre has opened in London, women with disabilities have formed self-help and campaigning groups and many articles and anthologies on women's health are now in print.

The women's movement has gone beyond a trend to become the way of life for a now uncountable number of women. It is change by and for women created independently of conventional political structures. Its success is that women have done their own thinking and that they see the personal as political. It is not change through political statute imposed from above. The new women of the eighties are unlikely to collude with an establishment that expects them to function in any of the old slavish ways. It seems highly likely that institutions will have to revise themselves along more equitable lines. The process of revision now touches all aspects of women's lives. It is not reversible. As a visual metaphor of 'the changing picture of women in Britain', the Tate Gallery in 1983 bought a work by Rose Garrard. It shows the frames of Old Masters being broken apart by the smiling female 'models' who, contained too long within, are now stepping out.

Voting at a union meeting
photos: Mark Rusher/Report

Select Bibliography

Beauvoir, Simone de, **The Second Sex**, 1949; Penguin, 1972

Bradshaw, Jan, Davies, Wendy, and Wolfe, Patricia de, **Women's Studies Courses in the UK**, Women's Research and Resources Centre, 1982

Coote, Anna, and Campbell, Beatrix, **Sweet Freedom**, Picador, 1982

Coote, Anna, and Gill, Tess, **Women's Rights: A Practical Guide**, 3rd edn, Penguin, 1981

Coussins, Jean, and Coote, Anna, **The Family in the Firing Line**, National Council for Civil Liberties, 1981

Dyhouse, Carol, **Girls Growing Up in Late Victorian and Edwardian England,** Routledge & Kegan Paul, 1981

Eddowes, Muriel, **Humble Pi: The Mathematics Education of Girls**, Longman Resource Unit, 1983

Equal Opportunities Commission, Ninth Annual Report, 1984

Faderman, Lillian, **Surpassing the Love of Men: Love between Women from the Renaissance to the Present**, Morrow, New York, 1981; The Women's Press, 1985

Figes, Eva, **Patriarchal Attitudes**, Virago, 1978

Harding, Jan, **Switched Off: The Science Education of Girls**, Longman Resource Unit, 1983

Harman, Harriet, **Sex Discrimination in Schools: How to Fight It**, National Council for Civil Liberties, 1978

Kamm, Josephine, **Hope Deferred: Girls' Education in English History**, Methuen, 1965

Kanter, Hannah, Lefanu, Sarah, Shah, Shaila, and Spedding, Carole (eds.), **Sweeping Statements: Writings from the Women's Liberation Movement, 1981-3**, The Women's Press, 1984

Lowe, Marion, **Women's Rights** (pack of information sheets and discussion notes), National Council for Civil Liberties, 1981

Mackenzie, Midge, **Shoulder to Shoulder**, Penguin, 1975

Martin, Jean, and Roberts, Ceridwen, **Women and Employment: A Lifetime Perspective**, HMSO, 1984

Martin, Roderick, and Wallace, Judith, **Working Women in Recession**, Oxford University Press, 1984

Miller, Casey, and Swift, Kate, **The Handbook of Non-Sexist Writing for Writers, Editors and Speakers**, The Women's Press, 1981

Millett, Kate, **Sexual Politics**, Doubleday, New York, 1970; Virago, 1977

Mitchell, Juliet, **Woman's Estate**, Penguin, 1971

Oakley, Ann, **Housewife**, Allen Lane, 1974; Penguin, 1976

Oakley, Ann, **Subject Woman**, Fontana, 1982

Oakley, Ann, and Mitchell, Juliet (eds.), **The Rights and Wrongs of Women**, Penguin, 1976

Pankhurst, Sylvia, **The Suffragette Movement**, Longmans, 1931; Virago, 1977

Phillips, Angela, and Rakusen, Jill, **Our Bodies Ourselves: A Health Book by and for Women**, Penguin, 1978

Rowbotham, Sheila, **Hidden from History**, Pluto, 1973

Rowbotham, Sheila, **A New World of Women: Stella Browne, Socialist Feminist**, Pluto, 1977

Spender, Dale, **Invisible Women: The Schooling Scandal**, Writers and Readers, 1982

Spender, Dale, **Women of Ideas and What Men Have Done to Them**, Routledge & Kegan Paul, 1982

Spender, Dale, **There's Always Been a Women's Movement This Century**, Pandora Press, 1983

Stanworth, Michelle, **Gender and Schooling: A Study of Sexual Divisions in the Classroom**, Hutchinson, 1983

Stones, Rosemary, **'Pour Out the Cocoa, Janet': Sexism in Children's Books**, Longman Resource Unit, 1983

Strachey, Ray, **The Cause: A Short History of the Women's Movement in Great Britain**, G. Bell, 1928; Virago, 1978

Study Commission on the Family (3 Park Road, London NW1), **Values and the Changing Family**, 1982

Study Commission on the Family, **Families in the Future**, 1983

Trades Union Congress, **Women in the Labour Market**, 1983

Trades Union Congress, **Working Women**, 1983

Trades Union Congress, **Homeworking: A TUC Statement**, 1985

Trades Union Congress, **Women Workers' Bulletin**, 1985

Whitelegg, Elizabeth, *et al.* (eds.), **The Changing Experience of Women**, Martin Robertson, 1982; Basil Blackwell and Open University, 1984

Whyte, Judith, **Beyond the Wendy House: Sex Role Stereotyping in Primary Schools**, Longman Resource Unit, 1983

Williamson, Judith, **Decoding Advertisements: Ideology and Meaning in Advertising**, Marion Boyars, 1978

Index

Abortion, 10, 70, 77, 78, 139, 154
Abortion Act (1967), 78, 154
Abortion Law Reform Association, 78
Academic Women's Achievement Group, 139
Adult education, 65–7
Advertising, 8, 70, 118, 124–9
Age, 9, 96
Alderson, Brian, 116
Amalgamated Engineering Union, 47
Anderson, Elizabeth Garrett, 58
Ante-natal classes, 68, 83, 79
Ashley, April, 129
Asquith, 22, 29
Astor, Lady, 31
Austen, Jane, 34
Auxiliary Territorial Service, 46

Babies, 78–83
Baldwin, Stanley, 31
Beale, Dorothea, 58
Birth control, 76–8
Board of Poor Law Guardians, 21
British Pregnancy Advisory Service, 153
Browne, Stella, 77
Buss, Frances Mary, 58

Cambridge University, 10, 59, 60–61, 63
Campbell, Beatrix, 118
Canteens, 47
Cartland, Barbara, 76, 121
Cat and Mouse Act, 25
Cavell, Edith, 29
Central Advisory Council for Education, 96
Charter for Working Women, 113
Cheltenham Ladies' College, 54, 58
Children's books, 116
Chisholm, Shirley, 122
Churchill, Winston, 23
Cinema of Women, 101, 139
Civil Service, 31, 42, 48, 49, 122, 139
Clough, Anne Jemima, 59
Common Cause, 20

Comprehensive schools, 54, 65
Conciliation Bill, 23
Contraception, 10, 70, 76–8
Co-operatives, 101, 113
Coote, Anna, 118
Crèches, 47
Crowther Report on Education, 54

Daniels, E. S., 77
Davies, Emily, 59
Davison, Emily, 26–7, 28
Divorce, 9, 70, 71, 74
Divorce Reform Act (1969), 70
Domestic science, 54, 56, 57
Domestic service, 62
Duncan, Lois, 116

East London Federation of Suffragettes, 28
Education, 54–67
Education Act (1944), 63
Ellis, Mrs, 35
Equal Opportunities Commission, 109, 112
Equal opportunities legislation, 65, 112
Equal pay legislation, 10, 112

Family, 9, 35, 70–91
Family Limitation, 77
Family Planning Association, 78, 153
Faraday House Electrical Engineering College, 49
Fawcett, Millicent Garrett, 16, 17, 20, 23, 30, 35, 58
Fawcett, Professor Henry, 35
Fawcett Society, the, 139
Feminine identity, 34, 35, 43, 50, 62
Figes, Eva, 96, 119
First World War, 28–30, 34, 35–43, 46
Frankfurt Book Fair, 140
Freud, Sigmund, 119
Fryer, Peter, 77

Garrard, Rose, 155
General Certificate of Education, 65

General Election (1945), 48
Gilman, Charlotte Perkins, 70
Gingerbread, 139
Girton College, Cambridge, 59
Glastonbury, Marion, 62
Governesses, 56
Greenham, 20, 136, 142–7
Greer, Germaine, 119
Gross National Product, 89

Hairdressing, 67
Hallinan, Hazel Hunkins, 112
Haslett, Caroline, 47
Health, 140, 154–5
Hide, Judge, 71
Holloway Prison, 22
Home Guard, 47
Housework, 56, 83–5, 89, 96, 104

Image, 114–35
Imperial War Museum, 38
Immigration, 70
Industrial Tribunals, 10
Inner London Education Authority, 65
International Labour Office, 48

Judges, 9, 102

Ladybird Reading Series, 55
Lancet, 39, 58
Language, 116, 121–4, 124
Law of Property Act (1922), 31
Lesbianism, 70, 74, 154
Lloyd George, 23, 25, 29, 30
Love, 75–6
Lovelace, Ada, 56
Lowe, Marion, 67

Mackenzie, Midge, 21
McWilliams-Tullberg, Rita, 63
Manpower Services Commission, 67
Manual work, 35, 39–45, 62, 100–101
Marriage, 9, 31, 34, 71–5, 83, 96
Marriage and Divorce Act (1857), 71
Mathematics, 54, 56, 59, 63

Matrimonial Causes Act (1923), 31
Media, 118
Medical schools, 49
Medicine, 58, 63, 70
Members of Parliament, 9, 43, 47, 48
Miller, Casey, 121, 123
Ministry of Labour and National Service, 46
Mitchell, Juliet, 124
'Moral right', 121
Motherhood, 34, 74, 78–91
Munitions, 36–41
Munitions Girl handbook, 44, 45, 50, 62

National Abortion Campaign, 139, 154
National Association for the Promotion of Housewifery, 56
National Council for One Parent Families, 139, 153
National Federation of Women Workers, 43
National Health Service, 10, 70, 78, 139, 154
National Service Armed Forces Act, 47
National Union of Journalists, 122
National Union of Women's Suffrage Societies, 16, 20, 22, 24, 29
Newnham College, Cambridge, 59
New Opportunities for Women, 66, 140
Newsome, Sir John, 96
New Technology, 63, 70, 103
Nightingale, Florence, 35
North London Collegiate School for Girls, 58
North of England Council for Promoting the Higher Education of Women, 59
Nurses, 102

Oakley, Ann, 10, 140
Observer, 29, 96
Office of Population Censuses, 96
Old age, 89
Open University, 66
Oxford University, 31, 54, 63

Pankhurst, Christabel, 21, 24
Pankhurst, Emmeline, 12, 21, 25
Pankhurst, Sylvia, 17, 21, 22, 28

Parliamentary Advisory Committee on Salvage, 48
Pay, 47, 94–6, 102
Penguin Dictionary of Proverbs, 122
Pensions, 95
Pethick-Lawrence, F. W., 50
Pethick-Lawrence, Mrs, 22
Private Eye, 119
Proverbs, Penguin Dictionary of, 122

Queen, the, 8
Queen's College for Women, 56

Rape Crisis Centres, 139, 152
Reform Bill (1913), 23, 25
Representation of the People Bill (1918), 29–30
Rights of Women (ROW), 139
Rowbotham, Sheila, 138
Russell, Dora, 11, 77

Schools Council, 56
Schools Enquiry Commission (1864), 59
Science, 54, 56, 58, 59, 116
Second World War, 43, 44–51, 62, 63
Secretaries, 110
Sex Discrimination Acts, 10, 54, 134
Sex Disqualification Removal Act (1920), 31
Single-parent families, 71
Slade School of Art, 63
Spender, Dale, 17, 63, 109, 112
Stephen, Barbara, 59
Stereotyping, 66, 116–35
Sterilization, 78
Stones, Rosemary, 117
Stopes, Marie, 77
Stott, Mary, 10, 17
Strachey, Ray, 22, 23, 71
Study Commission on the Family, 70
Suffrage, 16–31
Suffragettes, 16, 24, 28, 31
Suffragists, 16, 28, 31
Swift, Kate, 121, 123

Teachers, 65, 102
Thatcher, Margaret, 8, 93, 94, 102, 118
Times, The, 23

'Top People's Pay Award', 95
Trades Union Congress, 43, 109, 113, 139–40

Undergraduates, 54
Unemployment, 38, 43, 103, 109
University of London, 63

Virago Press, 142
Vogue, 129

Walford, Geoffrey, 116
West, Rebecca, 28
White, Cynthia, 129
Wider Opportunities for Women, 66, 140
Williamson, Judith, 124, 129
'Woman's Place' library, 140
Women Against Violence Against Women, 139, 152
Women and Manual Trades, 139
Women in Banking, 139
Women in Industry, 139
Women in Management, 139
Women in Publishing, 139
Women's Aid Federation, 139, 152
Women's Advisory Committee, 113
Women's Auxiliary Air Force, 46
Women's Consultative Committee, 47, 49
Women's Freedom League, 22
Women's groups, 113
Women's Health Information Centre, 155
Women's Institute, 43
Women's Land Army, 46
Women's Monitoring Network of Sexism in the Media, 135
Women's National Commission, 140
Women's organizations, 138–53
Women's Research and Resources Centre, 138
Women's Royal Naval Service, 46
Women's Social and Political Union, 16, 21, 22, 23, 28
Women's studies, 11
Women's Therapy Centre, 139, 155
Women's Trade Union League, 43
Women's Voluntary Service, 47
Woolf, Virginia, 55
Woolwich Arsenal, 30
Work: homework, 45; part-time, 45

Yates, L. Keyser, 38
Youth Training Scheme, 66